"Make sure you understand that this is not the end, but the beginning of a new era and a new world and a new understanding. The need to prepare is now, right before the birth of this new era."

Mother Mary

MARY'S
MESSAGE
TO
THE
WORLD

"The message and specific prophecies given in Mary's Message to the World should be read by people of all faiths. I have added Annie Kirkwood's book to my 'top five' recommended book list."

Gordon-Michael Scallion
Author of the "Earth Changes Report"
Matrix Institute, Westmoreland, New Hampshire

"I have read and shared this book widely. All are impressed with the accuracy of the messages. It is indeed a book of the greatest importance for humanity in this age."

Most Rev. Frank R. Bugge
Australian Archdiocese, Church of Antioch

We would like to thank our friends and family
who encouraged and supported us
in turning Mary's messages into a book,
especially Kit Tremaine, Paul Clemens, Stan Padilla,
Jean and Carl Foster, Kit Adams, Marta Welge, Sarah Alice,
and our children.

MARY'S MESSAGE TO THE WORLD

As Sent by
Mary,
the Mother of Jesus
to
Her Messenger

Annie Kirkwood

Compiled by
Byron Kirkwood

BLUE DOLPHIN

Copyright © 1991 Annie Kirkwood
All rights reserved.

First edition, May 1991
Second printing, October 1991
Third printing, April 1992
Fourth printing, August 1992
Fifth printing, October, 1992

For further information, and
for correspondence to the author, address
Blue Dolphin Publishing, Inc., P.O. Box 1908, Nevada City, CA 95959

ISBN: 0-931892-66-X

Declaration: Mother Mary intends her message to reach all peoples of the earth. It is hereby stated that the messages contained in this book must be understood not as words spoken directly by Our Lady, but received, in the form of "interior locutions," by Annie Kirkwood. For the sake of Catholics, this publication is in conformity with the directives published by Pope Paul VI on the 14th of October, 1966 regarding new apparitions, revelations, prophecies, miracles, etc.

Library of Congress Cataloguing-in-Publication Data

Mary, Blessed Virgin, Saint (Spirit)
    Mary's message to the world : as sent by Mary, the mother of Jesus / received
by Annie Kirkwood : compiled by Byron Kirkwood
        p. cm.
    ISBN 0-931892-66-X : $12.95
    1. Mary, Blessed Virgin, Saint (Spirit)—Prophecies—Miscellanea. 2. Spirit
writings. 3. Twentieth century—Forecasts. I. Kirkwood, Annie, 1937– .
II. Kirkwood, Byron. III. Title.
BF1311.M42M37 1991
133.9'3—dc20   91-11517
                                                                        CIP

Cover illustration: Stan Padilla

Also available in German translation (Christa Falk Verlag) from Blue Dolphin
Audio tapes of *Mary's Message* available early 1993.

Printed in the United States of America by
Blue Dolphin Press, Grass Valley, California

9   8   7   6   5   20M

Table of Contents

Introduction: Annie's Story

Byron, Annie's husband, together with Annie and the editors feel it necessary to explain some of the background, and to address some of the issues which this book poses.

MARY'S MESSAGE TO THE WORLD contains a powerful message and warning to people on earth. This is the same message, in book form, that is being received by the children in Yugoslavia, several people in Lubbock, Texas, and others around the world.

Mary wants people to know of the coming earth changes over the next ten years, and to have time to prepare for these changes. Some of these predictions are happening even as this information is being received. Mary warns of changes in our weather patterns that will include huge storms, earthquakes, volcanic eruptions, and the eventual turning of the earth onto its side.

This doom and gloom, however, is not the real message of the book, but is intended to give validity to the message as the events happen. The real message is how to find God in our heart and mind, how to live our lives more fully conscious of our presence and purpose here on earth, and how to prepare ourselves for our re-entry into the spirit world after physical death.

When we first encounter this text, we become aware that Mother Mary has blessed this woman, Annie, with most wonderful visitations, surrounding her with many angelic beings and special occurrences. Yet Mary has not come here to dazzle us with miracles, but to speak directly and sincerely to our hearts.

We may well question the authenticity and reliability of these messages. Simply read what Mary has said, and judge for yourself.

Basically, Mother Mary communicates to Annie "strongly" through the mind, and Annie "hears" internally what Mary says. Under Mary's guidance, Annie's husband, Byron, helped compile the information. While these unusual events were happening, Byron encouraged Annie to write down Mary's dictation using the computer. Byron then coordinated the messages into chapters according to their topics, and sorted them semi-chronologically within the chapters.

Perhaps because some of this information is controversial, Mother Mary asked Byron to compile some notes explaining why she chose Annie as her messenger.

The Choosing of Annie

When Annie came to understand that it was Mother Mary who was speaking to her, Annie protested, "I'm not Catholic! Marty (Annie's friend) is Catholic." Annie was adamant that Mary had to appear to a Catholic—not to her.

MARY'S MESSAGE TO THE WORLD

Annie told Mary, "I don't believe in the Virgin Mary. I'm sorry, I believe that you are Jesus' mother, but I don't believe in you like the Catholic Church does. Marty is the Catholic."

Annie repeatedly thought Mary had made a mistake. Over several sessions she argued with Mary that it was really Marty that she wanted to talk to, and kept telling Mary that she was not Catholic.

"Nor I," Mary responded. Marty then made the statement, "She's Jewish." This was the first time that Annie had realized that Mary, the Mother of Jesus, was not Catholic (something Mary has made clear in her messages).

Several times, Annie thought she was losing her mind. Annie is a nurse, and every good nurse knows that people who talk to God, or hear God talk to them are supposed to be locked up somewhere, right?

Annie is quick to point out that she has been talking to God for years, but didn't expect Him to talk back! Every time she thinks she is losing her mind, God, Mary, and the Brotherhood[1] let her know she has indeed found her mind. They have told us that this kind of talking to God is the purest form of prayer. Annie has been doing it for years.

All through this time Annie's main concern had been with her family and what would happen to them if all these predictions were true. "How could we prepare for such monstrous events? Where would we go if these changes were truly global, and who would survive? Why would some survive and others not?"

---

[1]The Brotherhood of God, also known as the Holy Spirit

Mary, in her message to the people of Earth, answers these questions, not only for Annie but for everyone on this planet.

Mary makes it clear that she chose Annie to carry her message to the world. Mary tells Annie,

> You were chosen because of your prayers and meditations, and your earnest seeking to know the Truth. I chose you, dear one. This always remember. I choose and I decide whom to give my messages to. You are the person chosen because you have lived many years and you have seen all sides of life on earth.
>
> You are also a mother, and as interested in your children's welfare as I have always been—but mostly because of your pure heart and your pure motives in seeking the Truth of God. I also chose you because you are not affiliated with any church or any organized religion.
>
> This person who is taking this dictation from my mind was chosen by me, the Holy Spirit, and by God Himself to bring this message of Hope and True Conversion. She was chosen because she was not looking for acknowledgment of any kind. She remains anonymous [Annie's desire was to remain anonymous, but she has agreed to reveal her identity to add credibility to the book.—Editor], and is working closely with us in spirit and in truth.

Annie has doubts from time to time about why she was chosen. Mary again answers,

> Your answer as to the credentials is that you were chosen because you are a simple and seeking soul. I do not have need of angels to tell this story. It will be among the common folk that this word will spread. The government officials are, as they have always been, too caught up in their own importance to give thought to any other kind of life.
>
> You have been chosen as carefully as the children of Yugoslavia. It was their innocence and their total isolation which attracted me to them. You are the opposite in that you are neither young nor that old, but of an age in which there is respect for

your word. You have had three children, a good career in nursing, and this is how you will present yourself. You have a good record to present. You also have lived in the world and know all its temptations and have lived in many worldly situations. For this reason you will have a good story to tell.

Mary is also concerned that her message actually reach the people of the planet Earth. She has sent her message for over two hundred years. However the Catholic Church has intervened in keeping her messages locked up, away from the people she is trying to reach. This is why she is sending her message through a person who is not affiliated with any formal church, but through "one who is truly seeking God in her heart."

I realize there will be many who will not believe your story. So from the beginning tell how I chose you for this work. I love all the people of Earth, and because of my love for the world and its inhabitants, I am concerned that my whole message is not becoming known in time for the world to prepare their hearts and minds for this great event.

Do not allow fear or anguish to enter your heart. I know you wish to keep your name unknown, and I am aware that you have never been looking for any praise for your part in this. I see in your heart one who is truly seeking God and the spiritual way—a soul who knows that her mission is not easy, but who does not shirk her responsibilities.

Tell the story of how I chose you and how you thought this could not be happening because you are not Catholic. I have not come just for Catholics, and I cannot be limited by cultural differences. Nor can you be intimidated in presenting this material to the world. Trust that I am free to choose, and I have chosen you to reveal this message to the world.

I will be using many different people to reach the world. Not all of them will belong to the Catholic Church. I will continue to appear in many places. My message must reach all people.

The religious and cultural differences between peoples are outer and not as important as they think. Tell people that if they wish to worship God, then look to the inner longings and desires of their hearts. Dogma and ritual is not as important as the worship which is done in your heart and mind. If it is of benefit to enter a church to pray and meditate, then by all means do so. Use whatever position, words, or place that enables you to pray. If it helps to pray the rosary, then use this method. But places, words, beads, and churches are not the issue. Your ability to commune with the One God is of utmost importance."

Annie's Concerns

Annie has been concerned about many things in presenting this material in book form. She knows that not everyone will agree with everything, but she is not seeking people's approval. In Annie's words,

"This is what she said, and this is what I received. To those people who will not believe, it is their choice and I will not try to convince them this is true. I can only pray for the reception of the message and that the world will heed this warning. Those who will believe and pray, will do so. Those who argue and disagree will never be convinced, no matter what we say.

"From the beginning I have prayed for this work. I have prayed that the words I hear be truth, and that the messenger come from God. I have prayed that this work be accomplished only if it is in accordance with God's truth, the real Truth. This is all I can do. It is all that Mother Mary requests of each of us, to seek with sincerity and with earnestness in our mind and heart to find Truth—to find our way to a close connection with our Creator.

"Those who will believe, will believe, and those who will not, will not, and it is as simple as that."

Annie also felt concerned what people were going to say about her credentials and how she was going to present herself to the public. She says,

"I know people have prejudices. But they need only listen to the content of what is being said. I do not want to deceive anyone or give wrong information. I have very sincerely prayed about giving this information out ... but I have no proof for the world. Take what you agree with and use it, and ignore the parts you disagree with. Mary will speak to the heart of each person who reads this book, and it really has nothing to do with organized religion.

"Mary is Mary. She is not necessarily who someone else might think she is. A few of my Catholic friends have told me that Mary seems much more human and real when she speaks to me, and that she is giving more specific information than what is being reported in Catholic publications, and that it is good to have so much of what she is saying in one volume. But, for example, they are very concerned about Mary not mentioning the rosary. I think she addresses the issue of the rosary. If praying the rosary is important to the person, then this is the method they should use. If the rosary is contrary to your religious beliefs, then leave it off. She is mostly concerned with all people and not just one segment of this country.

"I feel that the people who are ready for this message are the ones who will find the book. I believe Mary knows what she is doing. Just because she cannot be categorized into a certain compartment according to our beliefs does not make this message invalid. Sometimes we become too concerned with the side issues and forget to look at the real message."

Some people were also concerned about alienating Catholics. Mother Mary responded,

I have purposely not addressed the elements of the Catholic church because this message is not for one religion, but for all religions and for all people. I love the people of this world no matter what culture they live in or religion they believe in. My concern and love is for each person on earth. I have learned to love as God loves us, ignoring cultural and religious differences. One religion or one culture is not better than another. Each has its uniqueness and its beauty of faith and of creed.

These are my words to all Catholics who read this message: I come to warn the world of the impending future. My concern is for all people, and my love incorporates every land and every religion. Use the practices of your particular religion. In the Catholic church I urge you to pray the rosary because it is a good way to allow your mind and heart to dwell on the miracles and mysteries of God. It is good to pray daily and to follow the teachings of your religion. But be aware that the most important element is your faithful seeking of God through your mind and heart. It must go beyond the teachings of one religion and enter the lofty principles of Spirit.

To those of other religions, I urge you to follow the principles which will lead you into a close connection and leaning on the Father within. It will be through your inner heart of hearts and the inner mind that your prayers will rise to heavenly places.

As for the other lives which I and Joseph lived, this is the truth: every person leads one continuous life. It does not matter, as some churches think, if you believe or not. It is fact. Life is eternal. It is a gift from God the Father. There are no special rules or plans to follow to allow you to live eternally. It happens to every being. Many cannot believe this is true. In the early days of the Catholic church, this teaching was known and believed. It was abandoned for man's reasons and not because it was not true.

I will be appearing to many people in different parts of the world. I cannot be limited because I am commissioned by God the Creator. God is not limited. He is limitless and above all religions and dogmas of man. There is only one heaven and there is only one God. He is God to all people. No matter what name they use to identify God, He is the same. His love is for all people and His great gifts are for all people.

I wish for people to understand that God loves each one no matter what color their skin. He loves people. No matter what religion or what culture, all are children of God and all are loved with a love which is immeasurable. It is a love so great and pure that to catch a fleeting glimpse would heal your spirits, your bodies, emotions and your minds. God loves, and I love in the same manner because I have seen and felt this great love. Be not concerned with the elements of man, but with the elements of Spirit.

Pray, pray for the world—not only for your people and loved ones, but for all people and all nations. Pray for all religions and all cultures. We are all children of God, and all are loved equally.

Annie adds that "Mother Mary continually encourages us to stay strong in the knowledge that she is real and is helping us at all times. She says, 'Angels abound who are with you and committed to this Work.' To all who read this, **Mary sends her greetings and Love.**"

1

Mary's WARNING to the World

Mary, the Mother of Jesus, is sending this message to all the inhabitants of the planet Earth. It warns of the impending danger to everyone here and tells people what to do to prepare.

PEOPLE OF PLANET EARTH, listen to this message. I, Mary, Mother of Jesus, am alive and concerned for you. My message is to the whole globe and not only to church members. Listen and pay attention to my words sent through this soul.

Each individual living on earth will have some trials and tribulations to endure, and since these will be worldwide events, I wish to reach as many people as possible. For too long, my image has hung in churches and homes as one to be worshipped. Only One merits this type of worship—God, our Creator. There is only one place to find Him and that is in your heart and mind. Make peace with yourself and seek to find God in your heart and mind. Return to the origin of all. Return to your original starting point—God. We all have this in common, that each of us originated in God.

It matters not how you return to God. What does matter is the desire in your heart and the earnestness of your seeking. With all of your might and with all of your best efforts, seek to commune with God—Almighty and All Powerful.

The Coming Changes

The time is drawing near when you will be shaken and frightened, not because of any punishment, but to renew the land and the minds of mankind. The Earth will shake and will be moved by violent forces which will cause many to lose their physical lives. The process which will cause these earth-changing events has already started. The changes have begun and will continue until completion. The real tragedy during this time would be to lose one's spiritual growth.

The planet Earth is being bombarded with forces which will cause it to change its direction in relationship to the universe. As this universe grows and as the galaxies grow, there is a dividing and splitting of galaxies. These changes are universal. Some of these events started many millions of earth years ago. Now, the growth affects your solar system, and the planets will realign to new places and points. During this realignment, the Earth will be turned and shaken, and you will have many catastrophic events.

As the world turns and changes direction, many natural occurrences will be deemed disasters. Mountains will move; seas will be upturned; new lands will come out of the oceans, some of the land which is now inhabited will be inundated and returned to the ocean floor to be allowed to renew. These natural disasters have already started, but in the future they will occur more often and with increasing violence.

My desire is to warn you of the coming trying times. I wish for you to turn to God in your hearts and through your minds, for in this way some of you will survive these catastrophic events by renewing your spiritual values. Only in prayer and meditation will you find solace. Bring all your cares to the altar in your heart. Allow God to heal your hearts, your lives, your spirits, and your loved ones. This healing is your only hope, your only recourse. Only by prayer and meditation will you individually be led and guided.

Residents of planet Earth, heed these warnings. You are living in perilous times. Now is the time to come to God with an open heart and mind, filled to capacity with the Hope of God. This will be the only way to endure the trying times which you face. Far too long have you ignored all calls to return to your original goal. Far too long have you turned your backs on the spiritual element. The last few years of this century will bring many surprises and much upheaval to those on Earth.

How do I reach your hearts of stone? How do I reason with your closed minds? When will you listen to my warnings? I am appearing throughout the world. I will continue to appear in many diverse places. These apparitions will be for the sole purpose of warning you of the times ahead.

In the next few years you will see the hand of fate deal out some mighty blows to Earth. You will have earthquakes, volcanic eruptions, many large and damaging storms and tidal waves of unheard of proportions. Look for strange happenings in the sky, along with strange appearances of stars. The polar ice caps will begin to melt and to break apart.

In the last years of this century many will wonder about the reason for these events. Each incident will serve to remind you of your impotence. You will soon realize that you must look to a Higher Power to help you.

Pray and Meditate

People of planet Earth, pray, cleanse your minds of all fear, envy, jealousy, malice, despair, and of all addictions. Bring to the altar of the One God of the Universe a renewed conviction of His power and might. My hope is that you endure all things.

There are many predictions revealed in these writings which have already been revealed elsewhere. These are given for you to see and to believe. Believe in these words; believe in the Power of God to be with you every moment.

Renew your faith in good and in God. Look into your heart to find answers which will come into your mind at the appropriate time. Have faith in your ability to hear the Truth as it is spoken.

I plead with all people of Earth to spend time in prayer for yourself, your loved ones, and for your world. Praying is something each person can do. **Prayer is urgent.** Say the prayers you were taught as a child. Over and over God has said that praying is simply talking to Him.

What is it you do not understand? What is it you dread? What is it you need? What are your goals? How do you wish to be? How do you wish to be treated by others? Are you happy? Are you healthy? Are you living harmoniously? All these needs and desires are to be brought to God in your heart and in your mind.

If it is of benefit to enter a church to pray and meditate, then by all means do so. If you are better able to pray on your knees, do so. Use whatever position, words, or place that enables you to pray. Places, words, beads, and churches are not the issue. Your ability to commune with the One God is of utmost importance.

During the troubling times ahead prayer will give you calmness, valor, and hope as you set up the lines of communication with God. Come with your form of prayer and use it. Bring the setting which enables you to commune with God. Remember always that the most important thing is your ability to pray in your own way.

Sincerity is vital to prayer. God knows your deepest longings, your best kept secrets. He knows every thought which enters your mind. There is nothing hidden from God.

He knows with what sincerity you seek Him. In earnestness and in sincerity ask the One God of the Universe to help you establish lines of communication with Him. Your sincere desire to be near God will enable you to receive His guidance. God's ways are many, and He uses many different situations and conditions to reach out to you.

Re-read these words and find in your heart a new conviction and determination to pray and grow close to God.

CHAPTER 2

Mary's PREDICTIONS

Mary, the Mother of Jesus, is sending the people of this world predictions for the future. These predictions are only a part of the message that Mary has been sending for over two hundred years, but the message still has not reached the people of the world. She is doing this to forewarn us of the dangers that we can expect in the near future, to establish the credibility of this work, and for those who believe to have time to prepare for these events.

Mary is very concerned for both the spiritual well-being of mankind and for its physical well-being. These are only the predictions—the main message is to return to God. The details of the message and what we can individually do to prepare, are in other chapters.

*Annie was very concerned that the details in this chapter might not come true on the exact dates, or at best would frighten people. She was very hesitant to even include this chapter. But others felt that important, detailed information would lend credibility to the book. Annie asked Mary, and her reply was: "Annie I hear your concerns about giving the dates of the predictions. **Understand that these predictions can be alleviated and lessened with prayer. Pray*** *for the people of the world to turn to God the Father. In this manner some of the predictions can be eased. With more people praying more often and intensely, the severity can be lessened."*

The Predictions

1. There will be increases in the frequency and activity of earthquakes and volcanos, many in areas where earthquakes have never happened before.
2. Weather patterns will change dramatically all over the world. The winter months will be colder and in many areas wetter. The ocean currents will be changing and the magnetic fields of the Earth will be moved about. Barometric and magnetic fields will set new records. The animals on the land and in the sea will be dying off in great numbers, and many wild animals will become extinct.
3. The polar ice caps will begin to melt and large chunks of ice will break off and become a danger to ships and to seashores. The melting polar caps will cause the water level of the oceans to rise, changing the seacoast around the world forever.
4. There will be increased UFO activity. During the Christmas season of December 1990 there will be many strange occurrences in the sky. There will be unusual sun and sunspot activity. There will be unusual lights coming from space, like none which have ever been seen on earth before. Debris from space will land on Earth causing craters and changes.
5. Pope John Paul will soon return to spirit and another Pope will also follow in the way of the church.
6. Mary will increase her apparitions throughout the world.
7. There will not be a third world war. The countries of the world will be too concerned with sustaining themselves against the elements to wage war.
8. There will be famines in those lands which have had the most wars.

9. After the turning of the Earth, there will be two suns. This
    will become a binary solar system.[1]

The Immediate Predictions

These are predictions which have been given and are happening
while these individual messages were being assimilated into book form
(summer 1988 through summer 1989), up to about two years from
now.

Even as this information was being received from Mary, the
weather patterns had changed and the news media was reporting the
"greenhouse effect."

In her message sent on July 19, 1988, Mary predicted that there
would be earthquakes in India. On August 22, 1988 our newspaper
reported, "At least 550 die in quake. India, Nepal rocked by strongest
tremor since 1950."[2]

Mary told us about the changes that would be happening in the
weather patterns. During the days these messages were being received,
hurricane Gilbert occurred in the Gulf of Mexico and was described
as the biggest hurricane in history. Mary told us, "You on earth have
just begun to see the fury of these storms. The storms which will come
this year and next year, even though they will increase in size, will be
as nothing in comparison to the future storms which will lash the
globe."

In Mary's message on August 6, 1988, she told of unusual sun
spot activity and she also mentioned that the Northern Lights would
be seen further south this winter (1989) than usual. During the first
week of March 1989 there was increased sun spot activity (DMN,
"Intense solar flare may threaten broadcast waves"),[3] and on March
13, 1989 the Northern Lights were seen as far south as Chicago and
Dallas.

---

[1]This is a solar system that has two suns, instead of just one as we are accustomed.
[2]The Dallas Morning News, Monday, August 22, 1988, front page.
[3]The Dallas Morning News, Wednesday, March 8, 1989, "Around the U.S.," page 4A.

*On at least two occasions Mary told how the melting polar caps
would cause the coastlines to change.*[4]

*On Easter Sunday (March 26, 1989) Byron was adding some of
Mary's latest predictions to the book. Annie opened the Sunday paper
and handed him a section with, "The Rising Tide, researcher links
Antarctic ice to retreat of Texas coastline"*[5] *as its headline. It is
uncanny how the predictions we had already received were happening
as this book was being assimilated from the daily messages. These are
just a few of the events that happened in time to be included in this
book.*

*Mary's prediction is that the next major event will be an earth-
quake in Italy.*

*Throughout the receiving of these messages and the assimilation
of the messages into book form, Annie has had a problem with the
predictions. She feels responsible for them. She doesn't want to mislead
anyone. She had read a book by another woman who had received a
similar message, but this woman's predictions didn't come true at the
appointed time. Annie doesn't want it to appear that she has made
false prophesy.*

*When she explained this to Mary, Mary said, "These are not
your predictions, they are mine. These words are my words and I have
merely sent them through you. Be aware that I take full responsibility
for these predictions. They will certainly happen as foretold."*

In Mary's own words: Just as this summer season has
been unusual for those of you in the top half of the globe, so
will the winter season be unusual. There will be snowfall in
places which have not often had snow. And in those places
which usually have much snow, it will be below average.

The ocean currents are now churning and just beginning
to change their direction. The British Islands will most likely be

---

[4]From the messages sent on July 22, Sept. 8, 1988 and Feb. 21, 1989.
[5]*The Dallas Morning News*, (Easter) Sunday, March 26, 1989, "Texas & Southwest"
section, page 37A.

the first to notice the changing currents. The people of these isles will experience much wetness and more cold than usual.

Look at the globe as a huge ball filled with water. If you could begin to stir the inner water you would be able to see the changes which will be occurring on earth, for the core of the Earth has started to spin and churn. Visualize this ball as its center begins to spin. At first the surface would not feel any effects, but as the spinning became more pronounced you could see the wobbling the ball makes. This wobbling is what will cause the ocean currents to flow in different patterns.

These changes in the ocean currents will affect every shoreline. The fish and mammals will be confused and some will act differently. The tides will become out of sync. There will be so many changes in the weather and oceans that the government officials will have to notice.

The planet is already beginning to have some violent reactions to inner stirring which is occurring deep in its core. All of nature will be in an upheaval from now on. Many new records will be set, many unusual events will be reported.

The fact that they are not publicized does not mean they are not happening. It simply means that those in authority are not willing to admit they do not have the answers.

This winter (1989) look for the Northern Lights to be seen further south than usual. The sights and signs from the sky will include this phenomena. There will also be reports of unusual sun activity. The stars will be giving off different beams which will be picked up by your scientists. There will be unusual meteor showers, brilliant lights coming from outer space, which cannot be identified by your learned ones.

Also those civilizations which are on other planets will be appearing in record numbers. More and more people will see them and photographs will be taken by high ranking officials.

World hunger will be increasing, worldwide damaging winds will occur in many lands. The oceans will churn with out-of-season storms. Everything will commence to be strange to you on earth.

The earthquakes, which will begin on the Eastern sea-board of America, will take place infrequently. There will be small tremors this winter in the northeast of your country. Also there will be earthquakes in Italy.

In 1990, other earthquakes will be felt in Central America. Peru will have a major earthquake in the mountainous areas and it will cause much loss of life. But this is only the beginning. During these next five years many changes will come to Earth, but none will be so terrible as the ones which will come to the Asian part of this world. Earthquakes will be felt in Japan and India. This will be unusual, for in India there have not been earthquakes of this size for centuries.

The droughts which are affecting the world will continue. Those who reside on the African continent will be most affected, but other parts of the world will also begin to feel the droughts. The middle part of Russia will have floods and rains which will be unequalled in their damage. This isolated part of the world will be in the news and become known worldwide.

You will see religions begin to crumble and there will be derision amongst the church elders. The Catholic Church will begin to lose much of its power. There will be a call for the unity of all religions as church leaders find their numbers falling. This is because many will begin to seek their knowledge through spiritual means and through the work of the mind. The churches which grow will be those who profess to the world the idea of the One God.

These are events which will happen in the next year or two. You will see that this is all true when these events begin to transpire. You will see that it is all real. Put your faith in the One God and know in your heart that these messages are real.

Prepare your heart and your mind to receive more. During the next two years there will begin to be changes on the earth through the earthquakes which I have predicted. As I have told you, there will be changes in the weather patterns. Now allow me to tell you about other changes which will occur in the first years of the last decade.

1990–1992:

Your government leaders will be getting the messages of some unusual occurrences in the tidal flows. The oceans will begin to churn and there will be evidence of changing patterns in the way the currents flow. Some places which have depended on the warm currents will not be getting them as expected. The winds will become unsettled and unpredictable. There will be tornados in areas where there have never been tornados. Hurricanes will come out-of-season. These changes will be caused by the shifting molten masses in the interior of the Earth. Inside the Earth the changes are already occurring.

The polar ice caps will begin to break apart. There will be concern that the seas will flood many land masses. This will begin slowly and be unpredictable. During these years there will be changes in the atmosphere as it begins to act differently. In the news during this year, there will begin to be predictions about the coming events. There will be many who will still doubt. But some of the scientists will come out in favor of having research to study the changing patterns around the globe. Countries which have been hostile to each other will begin dialogue on this all important topic.

1993:

As I have told you, there will be three events which will affect the whole of the planet Earth. These three events will not take place simultaneously, but will have two or more years between them.

The first will occur in the year 1993. In this year the weather will be extremely violent. For a period of time there will be hurricanes, tornados, tidal waves of huge magnitude, and cyclones. The winter months will bring harsh, cold conditions. Each hemisphere will find this to be true. As one hemisphere is in the grips of a harsh winter, the other hemisphere will have torrential rains, mud slides, and floods. There will also be floods, mud slides, and torrential rains in all parts of the globe in this time period.

At this time, your government leaders around the world will become concerned. There will be speculation about the end of the world. Many will turn to churches which will not lead them to their own God connection. Many people will give money to these churches thinking this will save them. There will be prayer vigils to placate God. But this will not help, as this will be only the beginning of the end of this era.

1993 on:

There will be tremors felt all around the world. It will seem that the whole planet is undergoing an earthquake at the same time. These tremors will cause much damage around the world. You will still have worldwide news coverage, so you will hear about other parts of the world. Most places will have little damage and few injuries, but some areas will sustain much damage and even death from falling buildings and debris.

The world leaders will be in an uproar and will begin consulting amongst each other. **It will be in this year that the scientists will bring gathered data out into the open.** The nations of the world will be concerned, as they should. Much planning and many preparations for the future earthquakes will begin. The weather will become more violent and the storms from this year on will take on tremendous proportions. It will seem as if the heavens have opened an avalanche of storms.

In 1994, the state and city of New York will begin to be flooded with swollen seashores. The waters along this coast will rise and much of New York City will have to be evacuated. The evacuation will be permanent, but at the beginning many will think it is temporary. In this year, the polar ice caps will have begun to melt and that will be cited as the reason for the flooding. In reality, the earth will have already begun to sink in preparation for the major event. Along this coast there will be earthquakes and unusual electrical storms. The storms will intensify and add to the problem of the flooding.

The southern part of this country will have its problems, but they will seem minor in comparison. The gulf will rise and the state of Florida will lose much of its land back to the sea. During these mid-years, other parts of the world will be experiencing major earthquakes and mud slides. The lower hemisphere will have a harsh winter. Much snow will accumulate in places which have never had snow before. This will send an alarm throughout the world. By then the changing climate will have intensified and become noticeable.

In the year 1995, the giant earthquake will happen in California and the sea will recover that part of the country. The Pacific ocean will begin not to be peaceful as its name implies. The California coast will be racked by giant earthquakes. The giant earthquakes will also hit in other parts of the world such as Italy, Greece, Russia, Turkey, China, Columbia and in the Himalayan mountains. **This will be the year of the giant earthquakes.** The earthquakes which have come before will seem small in comparison with these giant monsters.

As these next few years go by, many earthquakes will happen in Japan in varying intensity. Japan will have already been experiencing many earthquakes and will not be concerned by them. The mid-Pacific islands will begin to grow as volcanos under the sea spout forth their lava. The South Seas Islands will grow the most. Those islands which have the large statues will come back to their original size and the land will be forested as it was in the past.

Now the rest of the world will not be without its torments also. **This will be the year of the giant storms.** The storms all over the world will be tremendous. Tornados will come out of nowhere and happen in places which have never had tornados before. Rains will be relentless in many parts of the world. The weather forecasters will be at a loss as to how to predict the unpredictable.

During this year, South Africa will begin to feel the tremors and the trembling of the Earth as it is off-centered. The orbit in the last part of this year will begin to change and it will have a slight swing in its direction which will be noticeable to your scientists.

The years after this will have all manner of occurrences taking place. In the last five years, UFOs will be seen almost daily. They will come in great numbers and will try to make your governments on earth understand that they come in peace. They will set up stations in areas of the world which are not as inhabited. There are but a few of these areas left, but high in the mountains and in some of the desert areas they will set up substations. On other planets, which are near Earth, there are already stations which have been prepared and are being stocked for man's arrival. In the last days, these will hold many people for survival.

The sky in the last five years will be very active and there will be many new stars discovered and seen by the naked eye. There will be comets which will come through your solar system. These will be new comets and some very old comets which have not been in this part of the universe in millions of years.

This is the year when most people will look to the church and to their religious leaders. There will be vigils and prayer meetings in which multitudes will seek to placate God. The churches will be blaming God and telling its people this is punishment for all the sins of the past.

Dear ones, these are not punishments, but are brought on by your acts and the acts of your ancestors. There has been a complete disregard for the Earth as a planet. The collective consciousness has been steeped in fear and anger. Somehow these pressures must be released. It is not God who will be punishing you, but the planet herself. Mother Nature, as you call her, is the planet Earth. She is the one who has been abused and ignored all these many years.

All educated people know that for any action there is a reaction. What you did not know is that this is true in all parts of the universe as well. There is, at times, such a lag time that you forget the action which started the reaction.

The pollution of the Earth is the cause of the severity of the coming storms and earthquakes. It is the planet trying to save itself, by fighting back. All the brains in the world will not be able to stop the onslaught of the Earth's rages. You cannot keep on polluting the seas and the forest without the planet herself taking a defensive position.

As the Earth gains ground in her fight with man, she will become the aggressor and will put you through much unnecessary pain.

In your country (America), the areas which will suffer the most will be the West coast as it disappears, and the East coast as it also takes its turn at being destroyed.

New York will not stand again as the giant trade center. It has polluted the world the most with its greed and its worship of power and money. This will be the year that the trading centers of the world will be destroyed by the planet herself.

More earthquakes will be felt, but perhaps not as severely as the ones before. Japan will continue to feel the earth as it trembles and moves. It will shake loose Japan's power center and they will be caring for their own and will not be able to take advantage of the world situation for gain.

The Indies will be besieged by storms, but these will not evacuate its population.

The African continent will find its long lost volcanos, which have been extinct for centuries. This continent will also be ravaged by famines as it has been before.

In this year, the people of the Arabian nations will not find the comfort of their fellow man, for every nation will have its own disaster to contend with. The people of the deserts will have too much rain and not know how to deal with the weather.

The Arabian nations will have their share of earthquakes and other natural disasters.

Not one nation will stand untouched, for every nation has added to the pain the planet Earth has sustained.

Through this whole sad scene will come hope and the people of the nations will begin to turn to their individual concepts of God.

Each man, woman, and child will begin to seek his maker. The attitude of the collective consciousness will have changed, and it will be an attitude of humility and fear.

I come to tell you beforehand, seek God and look for the answers to your spiritual questions ahead of time, for in these last few years you will be too busy maintaining your sanity and your individual lives.

Through all the disasters, commerce and trade will continue among the nations. The leaders of the world will band together and seek answers to questions which should have been handled in past years, but the cooperation and the attitude of togetherness will sustain the world.

It will be in these years that some of the aliens will suddenly appear to your world leaders and offer help. It will be as if the Angel of the Lord had come to help. But surely you who have the knowledge beforehand will see the workings of the whole Universe to save mankind.

With a new attitude, your world leaders will be ready to hear of ways to save the populations and of the coming turning of the Earth. The extraterrestrials, as you call them, will be of much help, but still your leaders will not want to give any hint that these negotiations are transpiring.

The people of the world will be in a mood of humbleness and genuine seeking of God. This is good, for through last minute seeking, many will be spared their spiritual lives and advancement.

God will help anyone who truly and sincerely seeks Him. He does not care that you have wasted, perhaps, the whole lifetime on earth. It's the sincere seeking of your soul which makes God happy.

These are truly the final years as you see, for the next big happening will be the turning of the planet Earth onto its side, as it juggles and shakes the oceans out of their beds and new ground is brought up from the depths of the oceans.

The new lands will appear in these last years. Atlantis will rise and become known.

There were two great civilizations who reached your era of technology in antiquity, Atlantis and Pacifica (Lemuria). This civilization was called Pacifica, as it was truly a peaceful place, but you know it as Lemuria. These civilizations also had to endure these tragedies, as you on earth will. This is not the first time this era of technology has been reached. It is not the only time the planet has been abused and neglected. In these old eras the people also became puffed up with their own importance. They also thought their technology had all the answers. Because of their complete lack of spiritual values, all was lost.

This time I have been given permission to warn you ahead of time. It will be by the prayers and meditations of a few that many will be saved. It will be by those who earnestly pray and meditate for all mankind that the technology and advancements of this era will not be lost for all time.

I will be appearing in many places in these last few years and so will other Angels of God. They will come to answer questions and to give advice. Many will think them devils, and many of your religious leaders will confuse the people and give wrong advice. They will denounce the spiritual realm which will show itself to mankind. When will you on earth realize the satans and devils have always been only in your mind? It will not be in outer guidance, but in inner guiding that these Angels will come to assist.

In these last years, those who are sincerely seeking God will have the advantage. They will already be on a first name basis with God and will know what it feels like to be in close communion with God. The Divine will become your lighthouse and your lamp. The Divine within will lead you to safe areas and to those places which will save your physical lives.

Now is the time to find the Divine Light in your mind. Now is the time to light the lamp of spirituality. Now is the time to come forth to seek God in your mind and in your heart. Do not look for God in any other place, for in these last days, many will say, "Over here!" and "Over in this religion is the truth."

The Divine door to God will not be any place except in your own mind, and to worship God, the door will be in your heart. You have read Jesus' words with this warning that, "In the last days many would rise up and say here and here."

But Jesus also told you the kingdom of heaven is within you. This is the truth as it was given two thousand years ago and it is still the truth today. Only within you can you find God and all the help you desire.

We know there are many theories about how these events reflect a turning of the consciousness and a tilting of roles between men and women. These theories are not true. The truth is that the very planet Earth will flip over on its side. All the land that has lain fallow over these last millions of years will take its place above the seas. This will be new land and the stars and planets will be stationed differently. Indeed and in truth, there will be a new Jerusalem, a new world and a new heaven. I am speaking only about those events which will precede the last turning over of the planet in my predictions.

The world will begin to notice many unusual events and there will be much consternation and perplexity among your scientists. They will never agree or make a decision about what to do for the masses. This is a great responsibility. No one will want to take the risk of being wrong.

My truth comes from God. This event was started many millions of years ago. By the time Jesus came to earth the spirit world was already preparing for this major event. There has been much activity in the spirit world for many centuries. For the last few hundred years many souls have been incarnating and trying to learn and practice all they can. Many on earth have recently returned to the spirit world and have immediately been reborn again. It seems that many want to be on earth when this event happens. There is not an event of this magnitude very often in the universe.

The universe is growing and expanding and will soon explode in new growth and new life. It is as if the whole universe has been pregnant for many hundreds of years.

The turning of the axis is the story of the book of *Revelation*. It is the story told in all cultures and in all races as the return of the gods. It has been told throughout eternity, for this is a major event. All the cultures of the world have had in their antiquity, stories of these last times, the last times of this era, and not of the world. Nor is this the end of the world. **Make sure you understand that this is not the end, but the beginning of a new era and a new world and a new understanding. The need to prepare is now, right before the birth of this new era.**

Many of my predictions are already coming true and are given to convince you that I tell only truth.

The earthquake in India (August 1988) was but the beginning of the earthquakes which will increase in quantity and in magnitude. The earthquakes which will happen in 1990 you may consider big, but they are simply a warning of those which will rock the Earth at the end of this century.

Japan will fall into the sea and that part of the world will become frozen wasteland.

China will have much land laid to rest under mountains of ice.

The islands in the South Pacific will increase in size and there will be new land which will produce many forests.

The continent of Europe will almost vanish as it returns to the sea.

The middle East will change climate and become quite cold and mountainous. The deserts will bloom and become virtually gardens of green growing specimens.

Much of the land which your country (America) occupies will be turned on its side and will all become a warm climate.

It will be quite different than it is now. Yes, I know you have hot summers and cold winters. Your climate will become milder and it will not be too hot or too cold.

The lands which will disappear completely will be the northeast and western parts of your country, England, France, Greece, and much of the middle East. The land which so many wars have been fought over will disappear, and no one will gain it.

Australia and that part of the world will become the major nations and will lead the world in peace and in reconstruction, for they will maintain much technology. Much of the land which is barren will then bloom. Australia and the surrounding areas will not suffer as much as some of the rest of the world.

The need for the world to continue in prayer and meditation is very important. So important, that I am at a loss as how to reach the general public. The world continues in its blindness and sees only what is right in front of its eyes. It will take a show of force to attract the attention of the Western part of the world.

In this age of technology, men have begun to consider themselves as gods. They prefer to believe in their own mind and their own reasoning, rather than in God's. They question everything and believe nothing. The questioning in itself is not bad. But when man will not listen to reason, he closes his eyes and ears. Mankind hurts himself.

God does not have need of your prayers. By praying, you do not add one thing to God's Greatness or Goodness. It is for you, as individuals and as collective man, that prayers are said. It is for mankind that these prayers are raised. It is for your awakening that you pray.

We of the spirit world are alive and we are already with God. We do not need your prayers. This warning is for each of you on earth today. The coming catastrophic events which will soon be on earth will awaken you to the power and might of God. The coming storms and tremors of unheard of size will perhaps make believers of you. The other signs of UFO activity and supernatural events will call attention to our plea to man.

Awaken and see what is about you! Awaken and see the danger you are already in.

The world is changing and there is nothing you can do to stop its changing. Man cannot control the weather patterns, nor can man control the size and frequency of the storms which will come out of the oceans. Man is helpless against earthquakes, which will be increasing in size, intensity, and frequency. Volcanos will come out of nowhere. Old volcanos will become active and alive with fury. These are just the beginning of the coming events.

These warnings are to allow you to rethink how much strength you as humans have. You should realize that there is a Super-Being called God, that there is Someone who does control the weather, land, oceans, skies and outer space.

The coming storms are beginning to be blown across the Earth as new vibrations approach Earth from the outer corners of the universe. These vibrations will cause many unusual happenings to occur on earth. The growth of the universe will be a major cause of the increase in the intensity and size of the storms which will batter your shorelines, your cities, and your plains.

In a few years the intensity of the vibrations of the magnetic field will cause many new and powerful reactions on earth. You have just begun to see the fury of these storms. Those which come in 1990 and 1991, even though they will be of an increased size, will be as nothing in comparison to the future storms which will lash the globe. The pressure of the barometric field and the magnetic fields will set new records.

The tidal waves will also set new records of intensity and strength. The coastal lands will be racked with violence. This violence which has been in your hearts these many years will be out in view of all. This is not a punishment, but the effect of centuries of hatred, anger and fear. The tensions which have invaded man's consciousness will be unleashed on the earth.

Sometimes I think you do not understand how this is all working together. The growth of the universe is constant, and it is time for the world to turn on its axis. These violent storms would not have to be incurred, except that there has been much hatred, anger, fear and emotions let loose in the atmosphere of the collective consciousness.

These last ten years of this era will be violent ones in nature and in the atmosphere. This is caused by the violence which has been let loose by the collective thinking of mankind during all these centuries.

There will not be a Third World War, for God will not allow you to destroy this beautiful Earth with your nuclear arms. You will be too busy sustaining yourselves against the elements to wage war. There will be much destruction of land before the turning of the axis. The forest fires have just begun, the hurricanes have just started, the tornados, the earthquakes, the volcanos and the winds will batter you to such a degree that you will not have the energy or will to wage world war.

The sun will also contribute to the destruction by performing in ways to which your scientists are not accustomed. There will be famines in those lands which have the most wars. There will be floods and other unusual storms which will make the world feel that it is under siege, and it is.

This is occurring for the future time, for in these last ten years, we cannot allow you to destroy yourselves for all time. The Earth still has life and a destiny.

Along with all this violence will come my apparitions which will be increasing all over the world. I will appear in many places and in unheard of places. The Church will not have time to investigate all of my apparitions. They will, of course, deny most of them because they will be at a loss as to how to investigate and categorize them, but through it all, I will leave many displays of the supernatural and the unusual for the masses. My message at every place will be the same:

PRAYER   MEDITATION   CONVERSION
RETURN TO GOD IN YOUR HEART AND MIND.

This is how I will be manifesting to all mankind. These are impossible times and it will take much faith and prayer to survive them. It will take the strong in heart and mind to withstand all the coming events.

(In this message Mary summarized what we can expect before the turning of the planet on its axis.)

The earthquakes will begin in this manner. There have already been several of large intensity in recent months. Each round of earthquake activity will progress in intensity and frequency. The amount of damage will grow. The quakes will begin above the equator. Then the southern hemisphere will begin to feel the onslaught. Even the Antarctic will have its share of quakes. More and more damage will occur around the world. The quakes will grow in intensity and feverishness each year. Atmospheric conditions will be affected.

The volcanos have already commenced. There is one volcano which is spewing lava daily and has been for some time. As the time draws near, other volcanos will begin to flow and spill much lava and create new ground. Volcanos will start to grow in places where there have not been any known volcanos. Underwater volcanos will create new lands in the oceans but these lands will be unstable.

As these last years progress, the sky will begin to darken and there will be more rains than usual. The so-called "greenhouse effect" will multiply its effects on earth. As the volcanos add new ash and debris to the upper atmosphere, the land will be under siege from storms. These storms will grow in intensity and unpredictability. The storms will be erratic in nature; they will come out-of-season and be of such magnitude as to be unimaginable. The oceans will churn and seem to boil in parts from the underwater volcanic eruptions.

These will be times of distress on earth for mankind. It will take the faith of prophets to maintain equilibrium.

The storms will come slowly and grow each year. The days of cloudiness will increase erratically. At times when you need rain, there will be none. When it does rain, it will come in too great of quantities and too many days at a time.

There will be extremes of all kinds. The unusual will become usual. The unpredictable will be what is predicted. The unbelievable will be commonplace. All about the land people will comment and lament the days which seem to last forever. The days of usual weather patterns and of calm, pleasant, predictable weather will be gone for a while.

Since the weather will be so unsettled, the patterns so unseasonable, the ice at the south pole will begin to melt in unusually large chunks. These large amounts of melted ice will cause the seacoast around the world to change gradually and permanently.

There will be discoveries of archeological treasures. Some mysteries will be solved, and others preserved. But as always, as some questions are answered through archeological means, others will be raised.

Magnetic fields will play havoc on earth in the last days. Machines will fail and science will not have answers. As the wave of magnetic energy which is traveling in the universe nears Earth, some unusual sights will occur in the heavens. There will be lights and sounds picked up from the furthest reaches of the universe. A different energy will enter the atmosphere. This will be one of the causes of the changing weather patterns.

The wave of new and different energy which is approaching the planet is bringing with it much debris from outer space. This debris will cause lights to flash in the atmosphere. Some of the debris will land on Earth causing craters and changes to Earth's lands.

In this new energy will be the makings of new stars and a new sun which will enter the immediate solar system.

The changes have started gradually and will escalate in intensity and frequency. The static electricity will increase and there will be major electrical storms.

I have seen the wave drawing nearer to Earth. As it does, the people will sense great changes in the air. The animals will begin to die off from changes which are evolutionary. Many people will blame other factors, and some of these factors are true, such as the burning of large tracks of forest, the extension of populated areas into the animal's domain. But in truth, it is time for an evolutionary period to come to bear on earth.

These predictions will be ongoing occurrences. The storms and the earthquakes will become increasingly larger in intensity and in destruction, but there will be some years in which the storms will become less violent, less of a threat. In these years people will say, "See this is it, and it is over. There was no turning of the planet. This was all a hoax."

But you dear ones, remember all things flow in the same pattern as the tides in which there is ebb and flow. All things in the universe have this pattern of the tides within them. Storms flow in this same pattern. There is forward motion and backward motion in all. Progress in everything is made in this fashion.

In releasing these predictions I come to give events which will transpire in your future. When these events are unfolding each person on earth will see and know something unusual is happening. In giving this information I am showing you that this message is true.

My desire is for each person on earth to connect to God and His Great Mind. I do not advocate the selling of property or moving about the world in order to avoid these events. What I say is that all parts of the globe will be affected. Every nation and every area of this world will feel the storms and the turmoil.

How to prepare is through your mind and heart. It is imperative that each person make a good connection to God the Father. Now is the time to pray, to cleanse your heart of all malice, fear, and angers. It is time for man to see that the important issues of life are spiritual, and not in property or titles.

Come, children of the world, come to the Father God with sincerity and earnestness. This is how to prepare for the future. This is where to place your emphasis, your value and your life.

Mary's Apparitions

(To convey her message to the people of this world, Mary has committed to making more frequent appearances in many places around the world.)

I am at a loss as to how to interest the human population in preparing for the coming changes which are already occurring. I feel it will take more disasters and more spectacular aerial events to get its attention.

For this reason I will be appearing in many places in these next few years. If my apparitions increase, perhaps the general population will take notice and question.

I come to give you the same message I have given at Fatima, Lourdes, Mexico and in many other places. My message has not changed and it will not change in the future. I am concerned with all who are now living on earth, for this is the "end time." This is the time which John foresaw in his writings of *Revelation*. He used those words which would best describe the events in language which was in use at that time.

Now I come to give the same message. There are some dark days ahead. There will be much destruction of the land and this must happen in order for this planet to continue to exist.

In Yugoslavia, for instance, the people are so tied to the Church that everything must go through the church officials. I wish to get the message to those people who are not a part of this church community. Everyone will be affected by these changes and everyone has the right to know. It will be through these writings that I send a message to the rest of the world outside the church and any religion.

I will appear in many places, but you will probably not hear of this. In one year I will cause a miracle to happen in Russia. Some of the people of this country have maintained their spiritual worship of the Creator in their hearts. This spiritual growth is being felt by their leaders. The new leader will allow the church to reopen and not punish the faithful. True worship is in their hearts and minds.

I cannot always count on your news media to relay the story of my apparitions. I have been appearing in many places, but in some countries I am not recognized. In some countries it is kept quiet and not told, for fear the people will come close to the church. For instance in Russia, I have been appearing in many places, but because of the commotion in Yugoslavia the government has put a ban on any more publicity. But it is spreading by word of mouth, for there are many who are questioning what is happening.

I will appear at the season of the celebration of Jesus' birth in different parts of the world. My presence will not be denied because there will be much evidence of the supernatural. There will be miracles. I will appear to the mainstream of human life, so there cannot be the denial of the past. I will be in many places and the people of Earth will know and feel this is me.

I come to plead for your minds and hearts. I come to warn of the coming turning of the planet Earth.

I will appear in Canada and in the mountains of South America.[6] I will appear in Korea so the people will have compassion for their own. I will appear in the islands around the world and allow the people of these islands to see me and to feel the great love of God. I will appear in the mountains of Europe and in the countryside. My presence will be seen in the middle East, near Jordan and those countries. I wish to warn the Muslim nations and to allow them to consider that Allah and God are the same Spirit.

---

[6]This message was received on August 31, 1988, long before we had heard anything about the young woman in Ecuador receiving messages from Mary.

(During the time this message was being received from Mary, the local news began to report of three individuals receiving messages from Mary in Lubbock, Texas. Annie asked Mary if she was indeed appearing to these three.)

Have I not told you I would be appearing all over the world and I will be manifesting myself in many different areas and ways? Yes dear one, this is my presence which is felt in this place. It is not only me, but the very Spirit of God Himself who is energizing the church. This church was chosen because the priest who is leading this church has prayed much and earnestly. More will be revealed by this church and more and more I will be seen in other countries of the world.

(August 15, 1988 was the day that Mary was expected in Lubbock. Doubting Annie (like doubting Thomas) again asked Mary if she was going to appear in Lubbock.)

Yes, this is one of the places I am sending my messages. Since so many have gathered together, I will be there and there will be healings of different magnitude.

(The Dallas Morning News, August 16, 1988, page one had the article, "Miracle vigil—15,000 gather to seek a sign from God— and some see it." The follow-on articles include "Study of 'miracles' sought—Lubbock bishop says special panel will be named."[7] And "Miracle probe may take years—Lubbock faithful insist events did take place.")

My apparitions will take place in many diverse and unrelated areas. I will be seen on mountain tops, I will be in the middle of the sky, and in the middle of the ocean. I will be seen in valleys, by the ocean, and near inland lakes. There will not be one place where I will not be seen by the end of this era. I will make simultaneous apparitions. I will speak to many people and tell them what I have given you and the children in Yugoslavia. The points of light near my apparitions will increase as more and more spirits take part in this warning.

---

[7] *The Dallas Morning News,* August 23, 1988, page 21A.

I will appear in your area (near Dallas) after the book is published. I will make it on August 15 to commemorate the day set aside in my honor by those souls in the Catholic Church. This will give time for this book to reach the public and for preparations to be made for this apparition.

It will be a major apparition. I will heal on that day and leave a fount of healing in that place.

I will continue to appear to men until the last day. I will be making more and more appearances. I will be blessing all who seek to find the Truth with God's blessing. He is the One whom I represent. His Love is what I give to all men. It is His Healing Power which I leave behind each apparition.

Events Already Reported in News Media

(DMN denotes *The Dallas Morning News*. Most of these are from our local paper only.)

Earthquakes

1. "Big quake rocks India, Bangladesh and Burma," *DMN* Sunday, August 7, 1988 page 27A, under "Around the World."
2. "Where quakes hit by the hundreds, but tiny temblors do little harm," *DMN* Sunday, August 7, 1988 page 4A.
3. "Strong quake hits eastern Canada." *DMN*, Saturday, November 26, 1988, page 14A.
4. "Earthquake kills thousands in Soviet Union," *DMN* Thursday, December 8, 1988, front page. This is about the earthquake in Armenia. (See also Dec 9 & 10 issues)
5. "Quake victims buried as Soviets search for survivors," *DMN* Wednesday, January 25, 1989, page 5A. This is about the Tadzhikistan earthquake. (See also Jan 24 issue)

Unusual Weather Patterns

1. "Drought attributed to jet stream split, Scientists unsure whether 'greenhouse' effect also may be responsible" *DMN* Sunday, June 26, 1988, page 22A.
2. "U.S. scientist says report censored. White House altering of global-warming paper causes furor." *Fort Worth Star-Telegram,* Tuesday, May 9, 1989, section 1, page 4.

Polar Caps

1. "Big iceberg breaks from Antarctica, Ross Sear floe is twice size of Rhode Island," with insert, "Changing the face of a continent." *DMN* (date unknown 1988) (Note: I think this was from the front page. It was continued on page 10A as "BIG.")
2. "The Rising Tide," "Researcher links Antarctic ice to retreat of Texas coastline." *DMN*, (Easter) Sunday, March 26, 1989, page 37A in the "Texas & Southwest" section.

Sun Activity, Solar Flares, and Northern Lights

1. "Intense solar flare may threaten broadcast waves," *DMN*, Wednesday, March 8, 1989, page A4 under "Around the U.S."
2. "Low Glow", about seeing the "aurora borealis in the southern 48," *Life*, May 1989, page 7.

Mary's Apparitions

1. "Miracle vigil—15,000 gather to seek a sign from God and some see it," *DMN*, August 16, 1988, page one. This is about Mary's appearance in Lubbock, TX on August 15, 1988.
2. "Woman's visions of Virgin Mary draw thousands to Alabama," *DTH (Dallas Times Herald)*, Sunday, December 11, 1988, page A-7. This is about Marija Pavlovic of Medjugorie, Yugoslavia visiting friends in Strerrett, Alabama.
3. "3,000 Catholics gather, hoping to see visions (of the Virgin Mary)," *DMN*, Monday, March 13, 1989, page 20A under "Around Texas & Southwest."

3

Mary and Joseph's Life Together on Earth

While we were receiving Mary's messages, she made several references to how she felt at a particular time or what was happening around her. I found this very interesting and asked Mary if she would tell us more about herself, Joseph, her family and what her life was like in those very important days of our Christian culture. The following was sent in answer to my request. It shows that Mary and Joseph were very human while on earth and had many of the same concerns as we do today. It also brings into play how they coped with the work of Jesus. They were very proud, yet felt very humbled by his life. It also tells how their love has expanded to include the whole world.

I WAS QUITE YOUNG when the Angel of the Lord came to me and told me I would be with child before I was with Joseph. For a while I wondered if I had dreamed this, if it was real. The only person I felt that I could talk to about it was a distant relative named Elizabeth who at the time was with child.

I had no idea she would be in this condition, for in our day news of this kind was not brandished about. In fact, when a woman was pregnant, she hardly left her home at all.

On my way to Elizabeth's home I ran the whole scene with the Angel over and over in my mind. Then as I neared the village, a thought entered my mind which stopped me instantly. I had not had any trouble from my parents about this visit to see Elizabeth. There was not one word of protest. Each family member had his chores, so when one was away the workload increased for all the family members. I concluded this must be the right thing to do at this time.

Upon arriving at Elizabeth's door she greeted me warmly and said some magical words which amazed me. She said, "Blessed are you among women, and blessed is the child you will bear! But why am I so favored, that the mother of my Lord should come to me? As soon as the sound of your greeting reached my ears, the baby in my womb leaped for joy."

Elizabeth and I spent a few days discussing the events which had happened to her and to me and how blessed we both were. Elizabeth had much information to give me about how to depend on God during this great adventure. She said God would speak to Joseph and he would become my husband. Every detail would be worked out with God's help.

In those days, I was a worrier and I just knew that Joseph would not want me if he found I was already with child. My worries continued: how could any man accept my story? It was unbelievable to me. How would I tell Joseph I simply was with child, yet I had not been with a man? Who would believe such a story? I continued to worry.

During those days Elizabeth taught me to quiet my mind and allow the flow of God's Spirit to enter my being and answer all these questions. She also taught me how to keep quiet about the things which were occurring in me and around me, until such a time as God would reveal the story.

Elizabeth became my best friend, and with much patience she taught me how to care for an infant. How to seek and hear God's voice. As a young girl, I did not have this knowledge, but with her help I soon learned much in the ways of women. The questions I could not ask my own mother, I could ask Elizabeth.

The days during which I was in her home were a respite and a rest. All the ways in which I would need to depend and rely on God and on Joseph were instilled into my mind.

Although I had always been very devout, very close to our Jewish heritage and religious customs, I learned the meaning behind many of these. I began to see God not as someone way off who only spoke to our ancestors but who could, in my day, talk to anyone.

I am now sure that it was God who taught me through Elizabeth. Elizabeth and I truly have a bond, even to this day, which is not surpassed by any love. Love bonds which you create on earth are very real and continue all your eternal life.

Upon returning to my home and with advice from Elizabeth, I told my parents what had happened, beginning with the coming of the Angel of the Lord and including all that had occurred during my visit with Elizabeth.

We spent much time in prayer and fasting as was the custom of our time. We went to the temple and said our prayers and made the appropriate sacrifices dictated by our religion. Then with much compassion and love, my parents began to prepare me, and themselves, to lead this new and wonderful life which God had ordained.

Joseph and I were married with never any thought except for the child which was growing inside me. We spent hours talking about why God had chosen us for this. We were afraid at times, and at times we were very comfortable with the idea of an immaculate conception and the birth of His Son to a virgin. It took much restraint for Joseph to put aside his needs in order to follow God's wishes. This was his sacrifice.

We pored over all the teachings of the prophets to see what and how it had been predicted that the Messiah would come. But we were puzzled that it had been predicted to happen in the town of Bethlehem when we knew no one in this community. We also could see no reason for going to this area.

Many nights Joseph and I would discuss whether we truly were the parents of the Messiah, or if this was an illusion or misconception on our part. As you see, we had very human doubts and questions.

While preparing for the birth, Joseph began his business of carpentry, building furniture and items for others. This is how he earned his living.

Then in the last months of pregnancy came the decree: each family was to return to the town of its ancestors to register. Since we did not have mail or phone service as today, we physically had to go to be registered. At this time we realized that we would be in the town of Bethlehem for Jesus' birth. We always called him by his name of Jesus, even before He was born.

Since we really thought we would be returning to our home, we only took those items which we needed for this particular journey. We were very ignorant of how Spirit works, but at the onset, we placed ourselves in God's hands and felt He would not let us down in any way. Joseph borrowed a donkey for me to ride to Bethlehem, but even that was not very comfortable. Being in the last month of pregnancy I was very uncomfortable anyway.

We took our time and did not try to keep the pace of the crowd with which we started out. There were in those days many people on the roads going back to their hometowns to register. Along the way, we met many wonderful people and were included in many family gatherings. At night, when we had to lay down along the road, it seemed miraculous that we would meet with a large family where there was always plenty of food being prepared without my help. After riding all day on a donkey in this last stage of pregnancy, I did not feel like cooking a meal or cleaning up afterwards. All I wanted was to rest my weary body. Not only was food provided, but nice soft pelts and blankets on which to sleep.

Every morning early, when we arose, Joseph and I gave thanks to God. Throughout the day we were constantly in an attitude of gratefulness for all the preparations which were made along the way.

Finally, late one night, we arrived in Bethlehem. Since all had been so easy on the road, we thought God would have a nice clean room prepared for us. When we were turned away from all the lodging places we became desperate, because I had begun the process of labor.

Joseph in his usual way, became riled and got angry with God for not providing us a nice clean room as he expected. Finally he returned to one of the inns and told the innkeeper of our situation. This man was very sympathetic, but there was not one room to be had in all the town. People were staying and paying to sleep on roofs, even in the cold night air. Every available place was taken. We were told that had we arrived just a few hours earlier we could have had a small corner of the kitchen, but not even that was available.

But, he said, he did have a barn. There was no one in the barn except a few animals. The barn was large and we could make pallets with the hay and rest well. If we needed anything during the night we could call on him, and his wife would help with the delivery of the child. Joseph asked only for a large pot to build a fire and plenty of water.

This the innkeeper gladly provided and even helped Joseph prepare our resting places and our evening meal. He brought out some bread, cheese, and had some tea which his wife said would help with the pain of childbirth. She did not think I would deliver that night, and by morning they promised I would have a place inside their home.

I ate a bite, drank the tea and soon was overcome with the weariness of the journey.

In the early morning hours I awakened Joseph, because I felt great pain and knew in my heart that Jesus would be born almost immediately and he was.

He came quickly and without much effort. Joseph cleaned us up and we both prayed and thanked God. It was in that moment Joseph remembered the reason we were in this lowly place was for Jesus' birth. He remembered the words of the old prophets.

The child Jesus was a beautiful child of light. Here was this newborn with his eyes opened wide. He had the most beautiful shinning eyes I had ever seen. He seemed to comprehend what we said. Immediately he smiled and followed us with his eyes. He was a marvelous child.

Jesus radiated light from inside. We recognized instantly that all our doubts of the past months were in vain. This truly was God's anointed child, the counselor and Prince of Peace. Peace seemed to radiate from his face, and it was glorious. In our happiness, we decided to keep quiet about this event and spend the night in a warm feeling of Divine Love.

In the first hours of sunlight, a few shepherds came to the barn to leave some sheep while they looked in the temple for the great birth. They said it had been given to them in a dream of the birth of a great King and they wanted to visit him. We kept quiet and allowed them to see Jesus.

Laughingly, we told them our son had been born on that very night also. They sat and talked with Joseph and were amazed that this was a newborn, because they felt he seemed to understand their words. Upon leaving, they told us we had a very special child for his face radiated light and knowledge. We did not reveal to them that they had, indeed, found the King of Kings. We were bound by God not to reveal this until the correct time.

We spent a few days in Bethlehem. Because there was such a mob of people who had come to register, it took several days of waiting in lines. Joseph said we should wait until the lines were shorter before we went to register. In this way I regained my strength and was able to feed Jesus and have him also gain strength. He was such a happy baby from the beginning. It was as if he knew this was his childhood and he should enjoy every moment.

Finally the lines became shorter and we entered to register as ordered. We continued in the barn, because many of the people had trouble registering and it took many days for most of them. The congestion of people stayed the same and we were quite comfortable in the barn. It was clean and quiet, whereas the inn was very noisy. There was much bickering among the children and mothers. The nights were noisy because of babies crying and men snoring loudly. We were very happy in the barn and in the cocoon of quietness which settled upon the barn every night at sunset.

The innkeeper's wife would not hear of me traveling until after the forty days which I needed in order to be purified. This was ordered by the laws of Moses. We took the time, because we felt that God had something else for us to do and we did not have a clear idea of what it was.

At the appropriate time of circumcision we took the baby Jesus to the temple. Upon entering the temple grounds there was an old man who quickly came to us and began to bless Jesus and to pronounce many marvelous words on him. We took this as God speaking to us though this man. As he spoke, there was an old, old woman who some said was a seer or prophetess and she gave a life reading for Jesus in which she foretold all the marvelous ways Jesus would help the whole world, and not only our people.

After the ceremony we returned quickly to the barn and talked about what had happened that day. Joseph was an impatient man and was ready to return to Nazareth to finish work he had left incomplete. We talked and discussed how my time of purification was not over, but Joseph was in a hurry and said we would pray and ask God how long it would be before I could travel. It came to Joseph that night in a dream that the time was not yet, that one more thing of an unusual nature would happen before we could leave.

Joseph, in his impatient manner, began to become angry and upset. I calmed him with words of wisdom, which I know came from God, for I could not believe I could speak in such a logical and understanding way.

When Jesus was approximately five weeks old, the next unusual event occurred. As always, the ways of God were very mysterious.

During one night there came three great men on camels. They were magnificent and learned men, who also were looking for the King who had been born in Bethlehem. They fed their animals, sat a while and rested as we gave them hot broth and bread. They began to speak of the purpose of their journey. We realized this was the event for which we had been waiting.

I brought Jesus to them and he awakened, and it was as if Jesus recognized them. They immediately knelt and praised God for giving Truth and allowing them to be a part of this great happening. That night they told us that they had stopped first at the king's palace looking for the new born King. They related how there was, indeed, one star which seemed to guide them to Bethlehem and to this very barn. But, they warned, they had a bad feeling about Herod the king. They feared our lives were in danger. They wanted us to go with them to their home where we would be protected.

Joseph said we would consider their kind offer and let them know in the morning. As there were now rooms in the inn, they slept inside the inn. During the night, as Joseph was in a deep sleep, God spoke to him in a dream and showed him the pyramids of Egypt and the great sea. He awakened me and we hurriedly packed. We took our donkey, Jesus, our small possessions and left without a word to anyone. On the road, we never told any who we were and used false names. We took care not to cause too much trouble or attract too much attention to ourselves. It was not done in fear, but in caution. There is a difference in living in caution and in living in fear and anxiety.

Jesus was a perfect baby who slept most of the way. The rocking of the donkey was as a lullaby for him. The trip surprisingly was one of great joy. In every town the way was opened for us by God. All our food and lodgings were prepared ahead of time and it all went smoothly. In fact, it was as if we were on a pleasure trip. The journey was long, but enjoyable. There was the sense of a great adventure beginning in our lives.

We could not send word to our family or friends for fear that we would be found, but through mental telepathy, as it is

called today, we notified our relatives. I notified my mother and
Joseph his mother. Soon we felt the peace in our hearts and
knew that they understood we were alive and well.

We lived on the outskirts of a large city of Egypt called
Cairo. There it was easy to hide among the thousands of people.

Joseph found work with a carpenter and was happy to be
once again working with his beloved wood. How he enjoyed
making things of wood. His furniture pieces were works of art.
And he gave credit to the owner of the shop always, for he did
not want to call attention to himself.

We prayed daily, meditated every night, and sought God's
counsel. Jesus grew into a lovely toddler and was very smart.
He learned to walk early and to talk at a young age. Because he
was very intelligent, we cautioned him only to speak to us in
our home and not when we were in public, so as not to cause a
commotion among the people. It was hard on Jesus, but it was
as if he knew we were on a great adventure.

We loved him much. He was an easy child to love for he
was very demonstrative and loved to give kisses and hugs.
Jesus was a healthy child. Other mothers asked me how I kept
him healthy, when all around us raged fevers and plagues
which affected most children? We simply said we were lucky
to have had a healthy child.

I kept to our home and did not promote too many friendships, but this was hard on me. Joseph was out among people
and had time to talk and to be with others. On the other hand,
I was indoors, so Jesus and I became very close. I did, however,
miss having friends my age. Still I was quite young, and many
of the other mothers were older and looked upon me as a
youngster. I was told over and over during these years, that I
was a child playing at being a mother.

We were in Egypt for three years, and in that time I taught
Jesus the ways of our people. He learned the prayers and the
reasons why we had our religious holidays. It was all low-key,
for we were still in jeopardy.

The house we lived in had a very small courtyard. It was here that, as Jesus and I played in the sun, I taught him of his people. I told him the stories of Abraham, Moses and Joseph, who had also lived in Egypt. I would tell him of his home in Nazareth. He learned of his grandmother's and of his father's parentage, that he was a descendant of King David. This made him very proud and he would play that he would some day free our people, like Moses, and lead them out of the wilderness as did Abraham. These then were the lessons and the way in which I taught him.

Remember that I was a very young girl of sixteen earth years when Jesus was born. We became not only mother and son, but also friends.

It was in Egypt that our family grew with the birth of James. He was not as quiet and congenial a child as Jesus had been, but he so loved Jesus, and it was Jesus who could sing to him, talk to him and calm his temper tantrums. There were two years and 10 months difference in their ages. It could have been more than that, for Jesus immediately became the big brother and took care of this younger brother whom he loved.

On the birth of James came the word that King Herod had died. Joseph however was cautious and waited until God gave him the word to leave Egypt and return to Nazareth with our family. When Jesus was three years and seven months, we left Egypt and returned to Nazareth to our home. Upon arriving home, our family came to greet us and to inquire as to what and where we had been all these years.

The grandparents were thrilled with our children and especially Jesus. Jesus was very much ahead of his years. He knew the stories of our religion and the words of our prophets, to the amazement of our family and friends.

During the year after our return to Nazareth, Joseph's father took charge of Jesus. Grandfather taught him much of the writings of our religion, the whys and how comes we had feast days—how these observances were representations of events which had occurred to our people in the past.

Jesus loved to listen and to question his grandfather. Soon Grandfather was taking Jesus everywhere with him. Joseph and I talked to Jesus and told him he was not to show off his knowledge or call attention to himself. Jesus questioned this and we explained that there was a great work for him to do later. But for now, he was to keep quiet and learn all he could.

In school Jesus excelled and was soon passed on to upper classes of learning. He was an obedient child and simply showed his curiosity and inquisitiveness.

Now, all this sounds like Jesus did not play and romp with his peers and brothers. That was not so. He was very much a boy and enjoyed running, skipping and playing with the others into the twilight hours. As soon as the first star came out, Jesus was once again looking into the skies and wondering what this was all about. He questioned us about the skies and the stars. What were they made of? Why were they put in place? He was seeking answers to the same questions which some of the young have today.

As our family grew, more and more children arrived. I had less and less time to spend with Jesus, but he was always near and seemed to understand. There were times when I would be sitting out in the yard preparing vegetables or meats for a meal, and Jesus would come and sit beside me.

He asked again and again about his birth, about how the Angel of God had spoken to me. We also talked much about our concept of God, what was written in our scrolls about God. He taught his younger brothers to be dependable and honest, as was Joseph.

When he was six years old, Jesus began to work with Joseph in the carpenter shop. At first he cleaned and swept, then he was given small jobs to do, sanding or learning to weave the seats and backs of chairs.

Jesus quickly learned all lessons. His mind was like a sponge and all knowledge was as water to be sopped up. Jesus loved Joseph and appreciated the love and the camaraderie which existed between them. There was a special relationship between Joseph and Jesus, which is not noted in your Bible.

At evening time, I could see them sitting in the early darkness viewing the stars and talking of God. There was such a closeness that they were at times of one mind. Joseph and grandfather Josh (Jacob) taught Jesus all they knew. He learned quickly what was available to him in our town.

Allow me to describe Jesus as a child. He was thin, but strong. He had much hair and it was the color of chestnuts. His light olive skin was tanned from being out in the sun. His eyes were very strange and at times were light green and other times seemed to be grey. I would describe his eyes as hazel now, but even that is not a good way to describe them. You knew what mood he was in by the color of his eyes. Although he seldom lost his temper, when he did, his eyes would become dark and menacing.

Jesus played with his brothers and sisters. He made up games to entertain the children when it rained. His quick mind brought many new ideas which his brothers and sisters also learned quickly. The children played tag, hide-and-seek, and tug-of-war, played with a rope. Jesus would spend hours working on toys for the girls and the younger ones. In the summer they would chase butterflies, pick flowers and play a type of ball game with a wooden ball that Joseph made for them.

Jesus was very normal in every way, except for his exceptional mind. He could memorize the verses and Psalms in record time. He learned very quickly and was interested in riddles and rhymes.

When Jesus was twelve years old, we took him to the temple. He could not believe the stories which were being told by the elders. He knew the stories were not quite being told correctly, so he began to correct the elders. He spoke with such authority that they were amazed. They asked Jesus questions and he could answer them with verse and with reason. This was the first time Jesus had disobeyed Joseph and me.

Joseph found him answering questions and brought him out into the courtyard of the temple to wait for me. As Joseph became engrossed in a conversation with other men, Jesus returned to the elders and once again questioned them. Joseph was quite upset with Jesus. We left immediately for home. We spent the whole night in prayer, asking God how to correct this child. How to reason with our young man who was approaching the age when the young rebelled against their parents.

We were concerned that Jesus would begin to call attention to himself before his time was ready.

That night in a dream, God spoke to Jesus and to Joseph with the same message. Both were told to find a school in a distant land. We were also instructed in giving Jesus as much schooling as we could. In our village he had surpassed all the others and was becoming quite well known among many in the surrounding villages. Joseph and I knew of a school which was in a land between Nazareth and Egypt. It was a school which taught the spiritualness of all beings. Joseph took Jesus to this school in his twelfth year.

He was there for two years and then returned to our home.

Once again Joseph and I prayed to God to give us some direction in preparing this child to do His work, as was foretold.

A distant relative came to visit in our town. He was a merchant who traveled in many exotic lands where spices and silks were obtained. He continually told of the ways and customs of other lands. At the age of fourteen, Jesus was apprenticed to this distant relative. He was to travel and learn all he could about other people and the world in general. This was our way of keeping Jesus hidden until God ordained for Jesus to begin his mission. We were not sure what the mission would entail.

During these years, when Jesus was traveling about the world, I prayed constantly. I meditated and did all manner of sacrifices to ensure Jesus' safety.

In the meantime, Joseph and I raised our other children. These children missed Jesus very much, even the youngest who was a girl.

The first child after Jesus was James. He was quick-tempered, loud, and boisterous. He did not learn as fast as Jesus, but he made up for this lack by his wily ways. He was a sly one and very astute. James became a carpenter. In his manhood, he had a lovely wife in Sarah, and a total of five children who lived. They also had three who died in infancy. They remained close, and made their home near our home. These grandchildren were the light of my life. They asked many times about my trip to Egypt. It seemed to them a marvelous thing to be able to travel. They asked much about Jesus.

David and Daniel were born eleven months apart and we treated them like one, or like twins. David was a strong and large built man. Even as a child he was large, or so it seemed because Daniel was so small and quiet. David was not really a loud, boisterous person, but he could sound loud because of his size. David was the type of person who had little to say, but when he did speak, everyone listened. He was a very loving man, and in spite of his size he was gentle. David was a carpenter and a horseman. He was very good with children and animals, especially horses. David married and had six children of his own.

Next there was Daniel, a sickly little fellow, most accident prone. He never married and helped in the carpentry shop as best he could. He was the first of our children to leave the earthly life. He died a short time before Joseph. I would say he learned many spiritual lessons from his infirmities. He remained quiet and loving throughout his life.

You wonder why Jesus did not heal him? Jesus wanted to, but Daniel was not of the mind to be healed. It takes the cooperation of the sick person in order to be healed. He was not in pain, just that through his illnesses, which were many, he was in a state of communication with God. Not everyone can be healed. This was an area of sadness for Jesus. He so wanted to help Daniel.

Then there was Elizabeth. I named her after my good friend and relative Elizabeth, mother of John. She was a tough little girl. She chased the boys and brought flowers from the fields. She had a strong mind and her father's temperament. She was quick to anger, but fast to forget the argument. This ability to quickly forget could be upsetting to others at times. Elizabeth could be so very angry one minute and it would all be forgotten the next. She would be ready to continue with the friendship without any rancor. Through her life she learned to temper her anger. She became a strong, caring lady. She had many children, nine altogether. They were the delight of her life.

Next was Jacob, who was named after his grandfather. He was also a strong and muscular young man. He had a very mild temperament and was happy with himself and the world. There were no known enemies to him and he never found any. Jacob was more inclined to farming and in his latter life he did this for a living. His love of animals and the outdoors were his source of joy. He had a large family of ten children. His wife was just as loving as he and was capable of guiding the children in their religious and spiritual training.

Then came sweet Ruth. She and Mary were the apple of their father's eye. Ruth was such a quiet and loving child. She loved to clean and cook. Her love was in the care of the house and in making special meals for our Sabbath. Ruth dearly loved Jesus and would take each word as a source of great information. Ruth was a very spiritual person naturally. She had four children, whom she loved dearly.

The children's spouses were good people who took right away to the family and to the work of Jesus. They supported our family and Jesus as best they could. Not one of the children's spouses was adverse to Jesus or to his teachings. I was well pleased with all these added children.

And last was Mary Martha, very quiet and very stubborn. She was much like her father but in a quiet way. She was a happy child because she had much love bestowed upon her. She reminded Joseph of his mother. She was slow to anger but also slow to get over her hurt feelings and angers. This young lady was, in her later life, a mother of six children. Her specialty was in sewing and in working to make beautiful cloths for the home. She was also quite a good cook, and took good care of Daniel, her brother.

Now then, we have given a good view of our family. My main message though is to every person on earth. To every individual who will bring his mind and heart to God, whatever his view of God is. To expand his concept of God, to expand his view of God's Power and Love.

(Here we asked about Mary and Joseph's childhood.)
I will be glad to tell a little of our family of origin, a little of mine and Joseph's childhood. Also, I will tell how I incarnated to aid those on earth to understand the marvels of the spiritual life which they had forgotten in their daily life.

As I said, I was sixteen earth years when Jesus was born. My family consisted of my parents, three sisters and one brother. My brother was named after my father, Hosyia. My three sisters were Martha, the oldest, then Hosyia, my brother, Ruth, then me, and the youngest was Delfia. We lived in the outskirts of Nazareth on what is today called a farm. We had animals, sheep and hens, and grew vegetables. The work was done by all in the family. There was plenty of work to be done, as we not only grew vegetables for ourselves, but also to sell. The hens, ducks, and geese were our main source of income, as they not only produced meat but also eggs. We had cows for milk and butter. My mother was known in town for her pastries.

Once a month we would all bake breads, both sweet and non-sweet, to sell in town. This was the highlight of our month. To go to town to sell our breads, geese, ducks, hens and roosters.

At times we had a lamb or two. During the month, before the Sabbath, my brother would take eggs to town as he had merchants who wanted all the eggs we could produce. And so was my life as a child and a young girl.

My marriage to Joseph was an arranged marriage. From time to time, the matchmaker would visit our home as he and his wife traveled about. They got to know the children and saw how we were developing in our religious beliefs, in our abilities in the home or, for the men, in training. Our temperament was noted and we were questioned about many of our likes and dislikes. It was a slow process which developed over the years of my childhood.

Our parents were consulted about what they had in mind for each of us. This was the custom of the day. We did not have a choice in our selection. We were always instructed that our best attitude was one of compliance. We were to accept the chosen husband and make the family proud by being the best wife a man could want. We were taught cooking, cleaning, sewing and all the domestic chores. Our duties to God and our heritage were part of our training.

As women, we were taught about our holidays and how to prepare for them. Cleanliness was very important. The preparations of our meals were an honor to God. We learned all these lessons, including those in which our talents were developed. My mother's talent was in baking. My sister Martha's was in making very neat stitches and in sewing. My talent were in the ways of healing and in caring for the sick. Thus everyone had her own specialty and it was developed.

Now this sounds like all we did was work and at times it did seem so. But we also played games as children and had our pets to care for. We loved running through the fields and chasing the butterflies and watching the streams of water as they passed through our fields. We could see the tadpoles and the frogs. We grew close to nature and through it came a great appreciation for our Creator. My childhood was not too different from anyone else's of that time.

One thing though, our parents truly loved and respected each other. Their love was an example to us of what a good marriage could be. We had neighbors who were not happy in their marriage. Their children were our friends. These friends were not very happy or proud of their parents. I decided very young that I would love my husband. He would be the most respected and honored man. I would teach my children how to love by example, as my parents had.

People were not too different than you are today. These were lessons I am sure our parents taught, but I am not exactly sure when or how it occurred. It was natural to be happy and to be grateful to God for His goodness.

God was a big part of our lives. From childhood, God was alive in our home and in our daily lives. I never remember Father complaining, but I am sure he must have, as he was very human. He was a very easy going man who seldom lost his temper. He was big and strong from the work on the farm. Father was a happy man and always singing, laughing and telling us stories with morals to them. Every day was a new adventure and a new lesson, he would say.

Mother was quiet and spent much time in prayer. She quietly led the girls in the lessons of making a home happy. She instilled in us the knowledge that the home environment was set by the lady of the house. It was the mother's responsibility to God to have a clean, well organized home, one which was truly a haven from the elements and the outside world.

My parents were devout and very close to God. He was not only the God in the temple, but He was a part of their daily lives. In our day, there were many who only maintained the Holy days as a tradition, those who did not put their hearts and souls into living daily with God. My parents, on the other hand, felt God's presence very deeply.

Now Joseph, as you can guess, was a town boy as his father was a carpenter. He learned his trade from his father. But as he is here, I will allow him to tell his story.

Joseph's Story

My story is quite simple. I was born in Nazareth and came from a very devout family. My parents were not as demonstrative as Mary's, however their love for us was in every word. Have you ever known people who could not say the words, but when they looked into your eyes you could see the love in their hearts? These were my parents.

My mother was very quiet and had little to say.

Father was the disciplinarian and the ruler of the roost. He was a boisterous fellow, happy and jolly, but he was also quick-tempered, and we children knew better than to cross his word. As quickly as his temper went off, that was how quickly he was over it.

Mother, on the other hand, held long to her angers and hurts. It took much cajoling to get her to smile. It was not that she was angry all the time or unhappy. Her ways were quieter and more serious.

We were four boys and three girls. The order was as follows: Abraham was the oldest. He could be described as more like Mother in quietness and in his ability to overcome sadness or anger, but he was fun loving and always had a joke or two. He married and his family was composed of six boys and one girl. He left Nazareth after he married and moved to another small town close by. They visited my parents frequently and brought the grandchildren with them.

Next to Abraham was another brother named Amos. He was a thin and sickly individual who never married. He was quiet and learned carpentry, but enjoyed working on smaller pieces of wood, making toys and small objects.

Then was David, quite a joker, very loud and boisterous. He was large and heavily built, even as a child. David married early in life and helped father in the shop. He could build very beautiful pieces of furniture. He would hand polish them to a sheen. His work was almost an art form. He spent many hours carving roses and flowers in the furniture pieces. This is why his work was treasured. David married and his marriage was not exactly ideal. They had four children, three of whom died before reaching the age of majority, leaving one child, a daughter whom he loved dearly. She was very spoiled and soon it became apparent that she would not find happiness either. No one could treat her as well as her father.

And then came my three sisters all in succession: Elizabeth, Dorthea, and Tanyta. These girls were the apple of Father's eye. He was crazy for the girls and so were we. He taught us to care for the women and to see that their needs were met with little effort. The girls were all very pretty and very cooperative. Never did one of them give mother or father one moment's worry. They were always with mother and followed her everywhere.

Then I was born the youngest and the strongest of the lot. I received much attention and love. Maybe that is why it was easy for me to love Mary and to care for her.

Father set a good example of how to care for the women of the house. He was getting on in age when I was a young man and he turned over the shop to David and me. I learned much from Father and David in the art of wood working. I loved the smell of wood. It had the smell of home.

I had been told about Mary, how lovely she was and how perfectly matched we were. My parents made all the arrangements for our betrothal.

I was twenty years old when Jesus was born. It was a big shock to find that Mary was already with child, and at first I had many misgivings. How could she do this? Why would she want to marry me? I thought some young farm boy had become involved with her. Then the Angel of Lord came to me in a dream and I understood, but understanding something does not make the task any easier. It was a year almost before I took Mary as my wife. That was a big sacrifice for a young man. But I spent many hours in prayer. I learned, through Mary, that God was a big part of our lives and would always be.

Mary could take me by the hand, talk to me and soothe my inner stirring with words of comfort and wisdom. She was always very loving and demonstrative. This I truly love in her. She is, and has always been, very special to me and now to the whole world.

Our marriage was one of happiness and joy. Our only worry was in doing what God had asked of us: to teach Jesus all we could, to see to it he received a good education in our Jewish heritage and in spiritual ways. It was with sorrow that I took him to the school away from home. I loved this one so much, but I knew I had a responsibility to God and to Jesus. When Jesus went away to the far off lands, I had to remain strong for Mary, not that she was an excessive worrier, but she was a mother. We comforted each other and through the years we built such a relationship that to this day it still exists.

On the whole, our children were good and did not give us too many problems, like some children did in those days, for then, there were thieves, murderers, and all kinds of evilness. Our children were taught by our religious methods to honor all the commandments.

At the beginning of our trip to Egypt, I was frightened and spent many of the hours on the road in prayer and in talking to God. What have I gotten myself into, I wondered? Will we ever return to our home? What will our families think when we do not return? I prayed for God to give me the wisdom and strength to know what to do and when to do it. In dreams the Lord would calm my fears. He opened my mind to see the beauty of His world around me. I began to get excited about living in another land and in learning to speak a different language. It is all a matter of attitude anyway, how you approach life. It is an adventure or it can be a great sorrow.

I had seen the quiet, unfeeling ways of my mother and the openness of Mary with her love and her friendly ways. I cautioned Mary not to call attention to us and to keep her smiles to herself. She was always to remain in the background of Jesus' work, I cautioned. This was what we were sent for, to support our son and to give him love and care.

Those years in Egypt we both matured and grew in the Lord. We set the pace of our marriage. It was easy, since all we had was each other. There was never any question of our loyalty or faithfulness. We had one goal and one cause: his name was Jesus. Our other children would simply be an added joy, I told Mary. They would be for our old age, as Jesus belonged to the whole world.

I died when Jesus was still preaching in the countryside, in the last year of his life. He was far removed from our family. This he did on purpose. He did not want us to suffer because of his preaching. He simply told us that we would all live and be together forever. At times his words were very strange to me, but I knew he was anointed by God, that his words came from God the Father, as Jesus always called God.

(Mary and Joseph have been together in other lifetimes since their life with Jesus. They have a strong love bond that will last for eternity. The following provides a little information about those lifetimes.)

Joseph and I had a very special relationship which was unusual for that day. We truly loved each other. Our love simply grew with each child. We enjoyed each of their personalities and their differences. They were all individuals with minds of their own. Their individuality at times led to some loud words being spoken. We always reminded them that we were one family and as such it was important to remain concerned with the entire family as a whole. This we stressed more than once.

When it came time for Joseph to depart this life, we made a commitment to be with each other for all time. We decided our love, which we were willing to have continue to grow, would incorporate the entire world. All people would be our children and we would love all creation, as the Father God does. We also learned much from Jesus and his teachings. Jesus, as the Christ, taught us many things, and we were happy to receive these teachings from him.

In my old age I lived with David and then with the girls and their families. In the last years I was unable to work and spent my time telling the younger children the stories I learned from Jesus. I also taught some of the neighbor children and the other grandchildren to seek God in their hearts and minds. This was the beginning of my message which I have, through all these years, continued to give to the world. I spent much time in prayer and meditation in my last days on earth. The children and grandchildren thought I was resting, but I was, in reality, communing with God the Father.

Assumption

I lived to the age of 60. Then I had a very easy death. It was simply a releasing of the body. There was no pain or any kind of unpleasant experience. By the time I knew it, I had passed from my earthly life and returned to the spiritual. I was with Jesus, Joseph and our families who had been with us on earth during that lifetime.

Other Lives

Now Joseph had already been studying in the different Temples of knowledge, light, and wisdom. These were mostly studies to freshen his mind on these subjects. There is no time or space here and so we do not have the time conception as you do on earth.

My next lifetime was as a nun in the Middle Ages. I helped establish the Order of the Sisters of Charity to care for the ill. At that time the ill were cared for in their homes, but as many were dying of plagues, some people had no one left to care for them. These souls I brought into a large rectory for care. There were several nuns, who took turns in preparing the meals and broths for the sick, in washing them and giving them water. The linens needed to be washed. There was much work to do, simply in providing water and meals. I dedicated my life to this purpose.

I did not live a long life. I also contracted a disease and soon was once again back in our true home, but the work gave a purpose to the church. There were many areas in which nursing services became available because of the church.

In another life as a nun, I returned and became one of the followers of Saint Francis of Assisi. He was a lovely man who had a tremendous amount of compassion. His serenity was contagious. His love for all life was an inspiration to many, and remains so, even unto this day.

In one lifetime, Joseph and I returned as nuns together and were close friends in this service, but Joseph did not like life as a female and has since returned as a man.

In this life we were very unknown and simply tried to lead a life of service to mankind. We always had in our hearts the teachings we learned from Jesus. It was these teachings which we lived and gave to others.

In another lifetime, I returned as a healer in India and wandered throughout the land from village to village caring for the sick. The people in this culture are very spiritual and yet you will find many who know nothing of the spirit. This is a paradox, in that you can have the most spiritual and the least spiritual in one culture. I was well received and given a place to rest in each village. Seldom did I sleep in the fields or out-of-doors in the rainy season. I spent time with the holy ones and learned. Also I gave them teachings as I had learned from Jesus, but they knew these principles already. I did enjoy talking over the ways of spirit with these learned men.

In India there are some old writings which hold much wisdom. These old writings came to the people from their ancestors in antiquity. This continent has always had many sick among their people. It is sad, until you realize that many of these souls chose these very conditions to advance in spirit and to learn their own spiritual lessons. The attitude of these people who have long believed in reincarnation is deplorable. They have simply resigned themselves to their fate and do not try to improve their lot in life. In today's society in India, there is no understanding that you can advance materially as well as spiritually, that these are all parts of the plan of God, that you do not have to give up one in order to have the other. This attitude of either/or is not in keeping with the Universal plan.

In one lifetime Joseph was a monk in Spain who came to this new world to bring salvation to the pagans. It was a mistake of the church to think that these people were not worshipping the same God. But their inability to speak the Indians' language and the oddity of their culture made the church believe these people did not know about God. Now in spirit, we know the Truth: that all people are truly seeking the One God of the Universe, the Creator.

Joseph came to bring not only understanding but compassion to these people, because the Indians had been exploited. It was Joseph's lifetime to learn and perfect his ability to have patience. The trip across the ocean was a trying one which brought Joseph many opportunities to practice patience. The inability, in the beginning, to communicate and understand the native people was another opportunity.

During this time Joseph saw these people as having much wisdom and much intelligence. He was instrumental in incorporating their customs into the beliefs of the church.

So as you see, we all have lived many lives and return to earth to practice the spiritual lessons in this three-dimensional world. We are given this opportunity to refine our souls and spirits. It is through this living experience that each of you is progressing or regressing. Your path leads you either toward God or away from Him. This is your choice and is your decision.

I would have all people pray, to give help and understanding to your fellow man. It is through your prayers for this world that the whole will be helped. Each life is a practice time, a time of polishing and refining our spirits. Learn all you can, and live each day in God's presence by prayer and meditations.

CHAPTER 4

The Subject Is LOVE

While sending her messages to Annie, Mary commented that the English-speaking people don't really understand the subject and importance of love and how it affects everything we do. This may sound strange, but for starters, English only has one basic word for love, while the ancient Greeks had two main words for love and other words that conveyed the concept of love. The two Greek words are "eros" and "agape." Here is Mary's explanation of Love.

L OVE IS A BIG SUBJECT which your language has condensed into one word. There are many aspects of love. Some of the words are esteem, like, enjoyable, friendly, caring, and yet these terms do not describe the different types of love.

General Love

General love, encompasses friendship, esteem, and likability. In this type of love you have friendliness and esteem for all life, plants, and nature, including people. It is a respect for all life; awe for the living, breathing, life-force which animates and brings all things to life. It is respect for humans as your fellow beings on this planet as living, breathing, animated life forms. This form of love is necessary in order to have a good image of yourself and others.

General love is an appreciation of all life and your entire world. In a marriage or any relationship, general respect and appreciation is necessary for a bonding to take place. A relationship which does not have general love, or the person who lacks this love, is one who will not be able to commit to or respect others. It is general love which gives warmth to friendship and the air of acceptance to the world.

General love is also the camaraderie which exists in friendships and for those who, for a time, become close, as in a school setting or when two or more lives become closely enmeshed.

General love is the love you have for a beautiful park or your own home; the warm feeling which comes over you as you see beauty or a familiar place; what happens in your heart when, after being away from home for awhile, you see your street or your city up ahead. There is a feeling of warmth, a sensing of those cuddly feelings of childhood.

This general type of love is an essential ingredient in your world. It is through this type of appreciation that plants grow and bloom, animals become pets and the home becomes the haven it was intended to be. The use of this general love is what allows couples to maintain relationship through the rough times in a marriage. It is the bonding or glue which keeps you in touch with family over long distances, or long periods of time.

Appreciation

Today many people have forgotten to appreciate the little things. The common is beautiful and can be useful if appreciated. To bring love and appreciation into your life, there must be a place in your heart where it will be welcomed.

General love says that *you* are a good and wonderful world. It says *I* am a wonderful creation. I love me, my talents, my world. It is appreciation. Appreciate your body, no matter what defects you see in it. Appreciate your home. Perhaps the door needs repairing or the window seat is old; show your home appreciation by loving it. How do you love it? Even inanimate objects such as your house or chair need appreciation. Inanimate objects function better when surrounded by appreciation.

Give thought to objects, such as your car, and show your appreciation with the care you give it. Talk to all things in your mind. Talk to your body with appreciation, and it will cooperate and function properly. It is by love that the body is healed, and through love the spirit is healed.

The body is a wondrous machine. It gives you the ability to speak, hear, see, smell, touch and sense the world about you. Look to the wonder and greatness of your mind which can take an idea and produce an item of use to you and to your world. Look at the motion which your body gives you. The ability to move from one place to another. See with those eyes the beauty of the world and your family. Feel with your heart the warmth and love which is stirred in it towards all living things. This is how to appreciate your body. Do not negate or belittle it. Give your body love and appreciate the life which is in it now, today.

Appreciate your family, envision the healing of rifts which have been caused by harsh words or unconcern for others. An appreciation for each family member's talents is also needed, in order to bring out in each person the whole of his God-given talent.

General love cools hot heads and brings peace to your world and family. General love stirs you to help your fellow man. It is by helping people that you are helped. It is by giving appreciation that you are appreciated. Include all people in your prayers for this world. Every person is to be appreciated.

Every person in this world is unique and individual—this is a gift to each person from God. You would not want to be a clone, just like everyone else.

Think on this. Seriously give it your consideration. What a dull world it would be if all people were just alike and all thought the same. What a dreary world it would be if everything was alike. A forest would have trees all the same size and type, eliminating ferns and small flowers which grow on the floor of the forest. How would there be any interest or any diversity? Would you not become bored with hearing your words and ideas repeated interminably?

What if this world were filled with only sparrows? You would never see a red bird or a parrot in all his colors?

Appreciate the changing seasons, for with each change come new colors, new views and scenes. Could you appreciate the cold without the heat? Could you appreciate the rain without the dry spells? How would you appreciate the sun without darkness? Every season and every aspect of your life is filled with wonder and beauty—just as the night sky is filled with stars and planets to gaze upon.

The love between friends and co-workers is a general love of appreciation—a respect for personalities. It would be dull to have your clone to be with all the time. The diversity and the differences in nature and in people are what makes life interesting. Love heals situations among co-workers and among family members. General love, as interest and appreciation, will heal not only bodies but relationships.

An appreciation for your neighbor, whether it be next door, the next country, or the next planet is what is needed in order to survive. Find the points of interest in your enemies, the common ground. All men are points of interest in the creation of God. This is the commonest ground there is. This is the basic element in all nature. If we were to break creation apart, we would find the Spirit of God as the most basic ingredient. We are one because God is One. We are all created by The One Creator. If this is the only way you can appreciate another, so be it. Begin today to appreciate all you find in this world. It is this interest in your world and in others which makes you God-like.

The love which is felt among close friends and family members is not romantic, but one of general love and warm feelings. It includes general love, but it also takes this feeling deeper into your heart. It is what you feel for a brother, sister or cousin. It is what is felt for your favorite toy as a child. It is also the love which is felt between a pet and a master. This type of love is one which can grow into very strong feelings of affection and compassion. It is what keeps friendships intact for years, the glue which holds families together.

Romantic Love

Romantic love: there has been much written in your language about this type of love. It is the love which makes money and sells items. It has been mistaken for sexual feelings. The romance which young people are so engrossed in is but a glimpse of Divine Love.

Romantic love is a conditional love. It says, "If you will treat me like I want to be treated, then I will love you."

The need to control all aspects of a loved one is not love, but possessiveness. Love is open, not closed. True love is given freely without any thought of return. Romantic love is very selfish and is only looking for an illusive feeling.

Keeping romance in a marriage is good. Know that romance is an illusionary feeling. It is a moment in time. It takes place in a setting, or in a place, or in the words of a song. It is the wonder of love which is needed in a marriage.

Mature Love

Mature love is the love a parent has for a child. It is the love an owner has for a business. It is the love you have for your possessions, like your home. Mature love is responsible. Mature love gives without thought of return. Mature love sees the defects in the other and loves in spite of, or because of, these defects. This is the type of love which is given in situations in which there will be a delay in receiving or seeing any benefits of this love.

Unconditional Love

Then we come to **the greatest of all loves,** *unconditional love.* It is the love one should have towards his children, for his partner in life. It is the Love God has for His creation.

Unconditional love is Divine Love. This is the love which can heal old wounds and hurts. It is the love which is only possible with no hint of selfishness. It is the love you give without any thought of reward or benefit. Unconditional love does not require any action to be taken, any rules to be followed. **Unconditional love is given without any restrictions. This is the way God loves us.**

The changes which are affected by unconditional love are always for the better. The person wants to change for the better, not so he or she will be loved more, but because he feels better about himself and others. Divine Love heals not only broken bones, but broken homes, broken spirits and broken personalities. The art of loving unconditionally is one which needs to be learned.

As infants we come into this world incapable of caring for ourselves. We depend on our parents to provide us all the sustenance which is needed to survive. As we grow older, if we are fortunate to have good, caring parents, we will be taught to love in many ways—to care for ourselves, our possessions, and our loved ones. But at this time, if we are not taught, we can become manipulative and have many wrong concepts of love. Love is not manipulative or engineering in any way. **Love will bear any truth, love tolerates, love helps, love will be waiting always to demonstrate its good will.**

As seeds need light, water and the proper soil to grow, so children need love. The child needs food, water, and the proper environment in order to grow healthy. The proper environment is not one of luxury but one of love and acceptance.

The child needs to be corrected in love and not constantly criticized. As the child grows he needs to be given direction, instruction in the use of his body and his mind. The child learns by example, by watching others as they relate one to the other.

Love is kindness, devotion, compassion, respect, friendliness, warmth, caring, appreciation, eagerness to help, smiles, hugs, softness, acceptance, reliability, tolerance, patience, trust, and other qualities such as these.

Love is alive, it grows as it is given to others. Spread love through your body, your personality, into your possessions, family, environment, city, government, nation, and to your planet. Love will maintain you in ways which are truly Divine. True love will not inhibit or possess you. Come to know and recognize love. Come to view true love as an asset and not a negative.

Loving Yourself

Allow love into your person. It is sad, that in this day and time, some people cannot love themselves. They think this is wrong. Many people believe the Bible says that to love themselves is a sin. This is the furthest thing from the truth. You are a creation of God: love God's creation.

If you think of yourself as a child of God and full of His attributes, you will respect yourself. As you view yourself in this manner, you will see how wonderful you really are. The idea of finding fault with yourself is wrong. This is not the way to correct wrongs in yourself or anyone else. Appreciate the life of God as it flows through you. In this manner you will come to think more of yourself. A good healthy self-image is what is needed in order to consider yourself worthy. When you can truly see yourself with kindness, compassion, patience, and tolerance, then you will love yourself unconditionally. First, **learn to love yourself unconditionally.** No matter what, love the life and the spirit which is in you. Love those things which make you unique.

When you are able to love and accept yourself in kindness and patience, it will be easier to love others unconditionally. Help others, but not by constantly reminding them of their shortcomings. It does not help to see only the differences in others and not their uniqueness. It is not bad to be different. It is an error to view these differences as bad. Find in yourself a common ground with all people. See the life which flows through them as the same life which flows through you. Tolerance, then, is easier.

Recognize that God's Love is the same for all His creations and you will see ways common to all people. It is God who is the glue which holds this and all worlds together. It is God's Love which flows through the whole universe. God's Love sets nature in order and allows the laws of physics to continue throughout the ages.

Maintain an attitude of awe for your mind, body, and spirit. Note the wonder in which you, and everybody, were made. Revere the world and in it find the wonder of God. Become compassionate for those who are less educated, less fortunate. Then you will view the world of God as He does. Open your eyes to the wonders in this universe and see the love which made all possible. Open your eyes to the wonder of the natural world and see how magnificent creation really is. Appreciate the love which unites each member of your family. It is love which holds the world together. It is love which will take us into the next age and the next world.

I would have all people first learn to appreciate themselves, their bodies, minds, feelings, ideas and thoughts. It is an appreciation of self which is needed today. Many young people compare themselves to others. Why compare, when what you are is individual and unique! You are an original and a masterpiece. There is no one else like you. Appreciate this uniqueness and individuality.

When you have learned to appreciate yourself, then look to the uniqueness of your fellow man. **See the difference as good, every person as an original.** When you are able to appreciate your own individuality, you will be better prepared to accept the individuality of others.

What has this to do with love? Love is the glue that holds this world together. It is the glue which holds families together. Love for your nation is essential to hold a nation together. Love is not only a feeling, but a nourishment to your mind and body. Love brings many dividends as you give it away.

Love the Creator of this beautiful world. Desire to know Him in your heart and mind. This is a magnificent Being! Respect the Creator—this is how to appreciate all things and all people. It is through God that all people and all beings are united into One Whole.

When viewing your world and your family with love, ask, What is best for the whole? Whether you consider yourself as an individual, or as a family-unit, ask, What is best for the whole: city, state, nation, world and planet? This is how to make decisions on how or what to do. Always consider the whole and then look for the best possible outcome.

These are some thoughts which I wish to share with the whole world and all people, not simply those who are followers of my son Jesus. I want the whole world to know about the coming events. I want all people to prepare their hearts and minds now. The coming events will affect every person alive on this planet. It will happen to the whole world, not only to the followers of Jesus Christ. As the Earth changes its direction and is set in a new place in the heavens, there will be destruction of property and of bodies. **Only what is in your soul will survive. It is the thoughts and feelings which you hold that will carry you through these major events. Hold in your minds and hearts the love and appreciation for what you are and who you are.**

You are Spirit

Remember, you are more than these bodies and this one life. You are more than your occupation or career. You are more than your ideas and thoughts. **You are spirit, and as a spiritual being you will return one day to the real world of which I am a part.** It is the unseen and unheard world of spirit.

During the coming crisis, many will return to the spirit world. It is to these individuals I speak. **Prepare for your return to your true home.** Prepare by appreciating your life and all you have learned in this lifetime. Come to God in prayer and ask for your blessing in this life. Time on earth is short for many, and now is the time to consider the reality of the unseen.

Love will be your main support in the coming changes. It is love which will save your family and your nation. It is love which will live on for all eternity.

Love Radiates an Essence

Love is like life in that it has the same essence, the same force. Love has a life of its own. Where there is love, it is much like electricity in that **love radiates an essence.** Love can grow in the right environment, or it will leave if not welcomed. Love's environment is acceptance, compassion, and simply allowing things to be. Love has its own vibrational field. It could be measured, if you on earth knew how to measure it.

Bring the love and acceptance of all humans into your heart. This is the first step in having love light your heart and mind. Love to you is an intangible, but in reality it is not. You can feel love as you can feel other emotions; therefore it is not intangible. Love has a vast spectrum in which it is active.

The Speed of Love

Allow us to view love as light, in that it is a measure of what can be. Love can be used to travel, in record time. You on earth now have a concept of traveling the speed of light. But you have never considered you could travel the speed of love. It is much faster than the speed of light. Also on earth you are beginning to find ways to use light to heal, to send images, and to cut away dead tissue. Love is similar to a laser. Love, when applied sincerely, can also rip away dead tissue and dead situations.

Divine Love is the laser of love. When you send someone a thought of Divine Love it is like sending a laser light of love into that person's heart, or into a particular situation. Divine Love will heal all ills: physical, emotional, mental or spiritual.

Think now of love as a tangible element of the universe. Simply because it is not seen does not imply that it does not exist. Love's effects in a home, nation, or even in one person, can be felt and seen the same way the effects of the wind can be seen. Love is more forceful than light, in that love will break down many more barriers than light. Love can be sent to another in an instant. Love will break down unseen barriers. Light cannot penetrate walls or buildings, love can! There is no barrier for love except that a person not want love in his life. Every person wants and needs love as one needs food and water. Love, however misguided, is needed in order to sustain life. Love and life go together hand-in-hand. It is possible to have life without love, but not for long.

Doctors have already experimented and found that children who are not loved in their infancy, do not grow as well as the ones who have received love. Consider an unloved child throughout his life. As a young child he becomes confused and knows in his heart something vital is missing. Soon this child will die, spiritually and physically, to say nothing of emotionally.

People who work with plants know the effect of love on plants. You as humans are more important and more precious than plants. You need love all the more to survive.

In the coming times when there will be chaos on this planet, it will be those who are united in love who will survive. It will be the survival of the fittest. Not only those who are physically fit, but morally and emotionally fit. The spiritually fit will not panic, no matter in what circumstances they find themselves.

I speak to those who will survive the coming times. Now is the time to prepare. **There are many preparations to be made. One is to love not only yourself, but the world.** If this sounds too simple, think what will happen where there is neither love nor respect. Everyone will be fighting to survive. It will only be in the spirit of unity that more will be able to survive physically.

Through loving thoughts you can communicate with the spirit world and with each other. Where there is a strong love connection there is a strong mental link. This is what it takes to speak telepathically.

Yes, you will be able to speak through love and to travel through love. This sounds farfetched, but it is true. You on earth have not learned it yet.

To learn to love, start where you are, with all who live in your home. Have patience and respect for those who are in your home. Learn with these people to find love and mutual understanding. Talk through your mind; tell them daily you love them and want only the best for them. In this way your ability to love grows.

As you progress, **include all people.** Nightly pray to find your true purpose in love; to be led to your true place in this life. In a few months, you will find that you are more understanding of the clerk at the store or the person in the street. It will cool your temper as you learn to appreciate and love more.

Always consider the love God has for each of us. He allows us to make our own mistakes and does not stop loving us. God does not punish you for anything. If anyone is punishing you, it is you. Look and see that your choices are the cause of your situation, whatever they may be.

Next, **progress to loving your enemies.** This is a hard lesson to learn. Begin by simply acknowledging the love and life which created these people. I understand the hardness of your hearts and the ignorance of your ways. It is my desire that all God's children learn to respect and to give mutual consideration, one to the other. Consider that each human on the face of this world is a child of God. We are all created by the same Universal Creator. Allow your respect for this Creator to soften your hearts. Bring into your hearts the love which is available to you at all times.

Love is like electricity in that it is abundant and is available to all. Turn on the love in your heart and in your emotions. Begin by loving yourself and your family. **Total acceptance**

without criticism is needed to love unconditionally. It is not love if you place conditions on it. Love is free and readily available as you give it away. Like a smile, love does you no good unless it is shared. **Love your world, appreciate your home, share love with your fellow man and with all living things in this world. This is what I ask you to do.** It is more than simply to love, it is essential to your survival to learn.

Spend time in prayer. Ask love to engulf this world and all people. This is my prayer and my desire. I want you to know what is coming and to prepare. Love is one of the easiest ways to prepare.

Love as Energy

Perhaps you do not understand how love is a force or an element, how important love is to your survival. Think on this for a while. Understand that through love, you will be guided to safe places and through love you will be helped. I love all people of the world. I want each person to increase their ability to love all people in this world and all beings in all worlds.

Love is an energy like gas or oil; the difference is that you create waste from burning fossil fuels. With love as an energy, you will not have any bad effects on the environment. All the effects will be good. This is an idea which is unbelievable, but just as you can send your thoughts of love, one day you will be able to travel physically by love. All man has to do is find the right combination to bring this element of love, as pure energy, to the knowledge of mankind.

This idea is not illogical and is truth. There are so many more ways to have energy supplied to the world than the means you are now using. The use of oil is causing many environmental problems for earth. It is also causing many emotional and political problems.

As an emotional problem, consider that you are laying waste to much of the underground. These spaces will not lie dormant for long. These spaces which are left in the ground will crumble sooner or later, leaving a vacuum in these underground caverns.

Divine Love is an energy force and is available as is electricity. It is "in the air," so to speak. You can send your thoughts on the wings of love. One day you will be able to send your body on the wings of love. This term "wings of love" is a metaphor and is not exactly how love is used as an energy.

Now dear one [speaking to Annie personally], I do not want to offend you or your intelligence, but I must clarify some things. I can only use those terms which are available to me in your mind. That is, I have to use the words I find in your vocabulary. So if I cannot find the appropriate word at times, I must revert to metaphors or parables.

You know of course that your mind emits currents of electricity. Also emitted from your mind are currents of vibrations from your emotions, such as love. Love is in everything and only needs to be recognized to come forth. But more knowledge is needed to use the energy of love for propulsion. The exact ability and know-how will come in the future. What I want you to know now is how effective love is, how powerful Divine Love is.

Divine Love is as powerful as any energy which you have on earth. It can be used as electricity for good or for bad. As fire, it will warm you or it can burn you. All forms of energy are this way.

Atomic energy is a good source of energy, except that you have not perfected it yet. You have taken this powerful energy and set it up to destroy. Also your technology has not found how to use all the components of this energy. There is too much waste. But with Divine Love as a pure energy, as with light, there are no bad effects from waste. When you use light as a tool, such as a laser light, there is no waste which can cause harm. There are some forms of light to which you can become

overexposed, such as x-rays, but even these do not leave the
bad effects that atomic waste and fossil fuels leave.

The Healing Power of Love

Take this thought, this idea and expand on it. See how the
power of love could be used to bring healing to this planet and
to all people. The smoke towers would be put out of business.
The nations which control fossil fuels would not have an advantage over the rest of the world. The giant waste problem,
which the world faces today, would be eliminated. There would
not be the need to bury waste or to pollute the waters and ocean
life. The atmosphere would be cleansed from the overuse of
pollutants. The forest would be saved, as you could also use
love to heal, warm your home, cook your food, and propel
yourself about the world. This is a gift which God has given
this world and all worlds. These are some of the new tools and
new energies which will be available to you in the new age and
in the aftertime.

Can you imagine what a pleasure it will be to live in a
world which is energized by love? When light and love are
combined, this could send all your technology down the drain.
It would all become obsolete. There would not be a need for
hospitals, prisons and institutions for the mentally ill. The blind
would see and the deaf could hear instantly.

Jesus used the energy of God's Love to heal all manner of
illnesses. He wanted you to know how wonderful God's Kingdom is. Understand that Jesus had to use the terms which were
available to him in that day, the words which people could
understand, as I must use the terms and words which are
available to me through this writer.

Dear children, open your eyes to the wonders which are
in God. See the wonder which is in His Love and His Energy.
Bring God's Love into your being and into your world. Love

will help you overcome all physical trials. As you enter the time of great tragedy, you will need Divine Love to fill you not only with energy, but hope and the knowledge that all things work together for good. It is this hope and love which will keep you from becoming too frightened. It will help to have this knowledge when you find yourself overcome by storms and the rumblings of the Earth.

Consider how wonderful it will be to have energy to use that is free and not commercialized. How wonderful it will be for all countries to have the same sources of energy. There will not be the element of a power struggle involved, as is now the case in the countries which need fuel and the ones which have the fuel. When this energy is available to all nations, it will eliminate the misuse of political power. It is this misuse of power which has caused so many problems in today's world. These kinds of problems happen when there is an exploitation of any kind.

Our topic is Divine Love as an energy, and this is the message which I wish to give today, that love is powerful in its properties, its uses and its elements. Love is so powerful that using a small amount of love, you can heal bodies, minds, and relationships. The ability to send thoughts of love to another is very powerful, not that it will give you, the sender, any power over the receiver, but because love will heal all manner of ills between you.

Consciously sit and radiate love into your home. This sounds absurd, but it works. Do you have a loved one who is ill? Sit by his side and think loving thoughts. This is the same as asking God in prayer, for a healing. God is Love, and as Love He is the energy which heals. **In order to radiate love, all you need do is become quiet in your mind and concentrate on the word "LOVE."** Think in terms of radiating love out into your environment. All these exercises are mental, and as such are very powerful.

Try these mental exercises to heal the Earth and all its people. I, Mary, Mother of Jesus ask you to do this. Help me send love into the world and into each person alive on Earth.

Love as Chemistry

Now, we have seen that love is an energy similar to electricity, gas or oil, but love is so much more. Love is a healing agent, as is light. Love is personal and is impersonal. In personal love you have the romantic and the family type of love. The friendship type of love can also be very strong and pure. But today we will expand on love as a healing agent.

Think of love as a warm feeling and sense the feelings of acceptance and care which surround your body. In this atmosphere of acceptance and warmth, the very cells of your body multiply. Where there is love, there is care. Care is what it takes to make things grow, even the cells of the body. Each cell is filled with individual particles, and each particle has a function. If any of these functions are discontinued, the cell dies. Now as one cell dies, new cells are made.

Your body, as the universe, is made up of chemical molecules which must interact with each other properly to keep order.

The molecules are suspended in love. This sounds perhaps unlikely and ridiculous, but it is truth! The suspension of molecules *is* love, and it is love which carries out each chemical process. Love is thus the unseen element which suspends and carries each molecule to its destination.

If the chemical process occurs in the body, it is called "body fluids," for that is how they are seen on earth. In the universe it is called "interplanetary expansion." Each molecule is carried and suspended in love, no matter where the molecule is found in the universe. Love, in this way, is a healing agent. The healing agents need recognition, and the calling out in your mind of love to activate and heal your body.

Love has a vibrational element of its own. It is a distinct and very intense vibration which moves the molecules along their individual paths. As you call on love in your mind, you set into motion certain vibrations and chemical changes as you think. This in turn causes the vibrations of love to scintillate and vibrate along each chemical current as the charge of electrical impulse is sent throughout the brain.

The love vibration carries the chemical changes along the paths of the neurons, and as they run throughout your body it causes all vibrations of love to begin to scintillate. The chemical elements in your body start to regulate and come into their proper levels. As these levels reach their proper amounts, you feel the healing energy of love. There is a period of time when these changes begin to occur and you begin to feel the effects. At times the effects are immediate, and at other times it takes a little longer to feel the effects.

Do you realize what this means? **God is Love!** This is a truth and is undisputable. Then it is God Himself who is responsible for the chemical changes and the carrying of molecules throughout your body and the universe. **God is in each cell of your physical body.** He is the regulator of all your body functions. Yes, I hear your question: why all the illness?

Illnesses are caused by many different reasons: unhealthy habits, unhealthy moods, lack of cleanliness, one's thinking and one's choices. God will not interfere with your choices, even if the choice causes you pain and illness.

The implications of this are mind boggling, are they not? You are the king of your world; you make the decisions for your body and your life. There are lessons which can be learned easier through illnesses. These lessons are spiritual. It is you and your higher self who make this decision.

The utopian life you on earth seek is your spiritual life when it is lived from the highest spiritual level. This is your desire: to live in complete happiness. It is your memory of the garden of Eden. This is what you seek to regain again. My aim in explaining love, is for each of you to expand your knowledge and your vision of the spiritual world. **My desire for you is to know how God works to preserve your spiritual life. How great His Love is for you, that each cell in your body is surrounded by God's Love.** Each function of your physical body is carried out in God's Love.

Consider that the physical body is transitory, not permanent, yet God's Love surrounds each cell and is active in each function. How much more active He is in your spiritual existence. Spiritual life is the real life, where you are even more special and dear to God.

Love is not only active in each physical and spiritual function, but in many more levels of function. You are many things, and many different elements make up your entire spiritual self. God's Love is a part of each of these functions and elements.

Some people have a problem in thinking of God as personal and yet impersonal. God is very personal and very much a part of you. Do you not see this now? Do you not realize how personal He is? How much more personal can He be, than a part of each of your cells, of each chemical function and of each mental function? How wonderful to know that no one is a clone or a robot. Every person is a special free being, capable and able to make all choices. Each individual is free to create or destroy his physical life, time and again. A clean slate comes with each lifetime and a new chance to rectify your mistakes. All events and all actions become lessons, even illness. **Even though God is in each cell and is a part of each function, He does not impose His will on you. This, dear ones, is LOVE!**

Can you love your spouse, children, or friends in this way? Can you say, "No matter what you do or what you say I will love you and prove it? Freedom to choose and to make mistakes is yours. Freedom to correct your wrong concepts or to find truth is yours."

No one has demanded that this writer begin her journey in search of the truth. This was her decision; she chose to seek God and to find the truth. When she seriously decided to find God's Truth, she set into motion certain operations and functions, both in her physical self and in her spiritual self. These operations, for want of a better word, have led her to read and listen to her inner self. She prayed much and asked God many questions. Then she demanded answers.

Her first concern was for her family, but then her family grew to include the world. What love God has for each of you, that He is always ready and waiting for a word from you. He is in constant contact with each of you physically, spiritually, mentally, and emotionally.

Take these words into your mind and heart and prove their truth. This proving of truth is through prayer and quietness of mind. Allow God to answer your questions! Listen to these words and question the validity in each idea. These are truths which are eternal.

My constant request throughout this book is for each of you to turn to your idea of God and pray for yourself, your family, and your world. I am Mary, Mother of Jesus, but it is God who created the universe and all the functions of this universe and all beings. I am not the one to seek for truth, for All Truth comes from God and is God.

Is all this strange to you? Ask God in prayer to give you the answers to your questions. Dear children of the world, you do not know everything. You do not know much! You have raised your level of intelligence and have attained much in technology, but you did not cause the energy which this level of technology uses. God did! With all your learning and with all your worldly knowledge, you cannot add one star to the sky, or change the rotation of the planet. Did you make electricity or merely find it? Did you make the waves which carry the images of your television or merely find them? Did you make the atom or merely find it? Take a good look at yourself and see the truth. Can you create worlds and beings? This is God's Creation and these are God's worlds.

All nature is created by chemical reactions. All nature is maintained by the same process. These chemical elements float in Divine Love. If your conscious mind knows very little of chemistry, think in terms of molecules, antigens, and cells for a minute. Each element of life is like a chemical changing. Each changing of chemicals brings new elements to your life. As you see, chemistry, mathematics and symbols are all matter of life. This matter is carried along into each new change by love. So love is a current as are the currents of the oceans. Each wave action of love brings changes and new meanings to life.

Take this same idea into your life as a total being. As you intermingle and relate with others, your thoughts are carried along by way of love. It is this reaction which impresses you as you meet someone for the first time. It is the acknowledgment of the sameness of mind. The same currents of love are recognized, and either you like this person or you do not. But since nothing is static and all things are in constant change, your feelings towards a person can grow into love and friendship, or can regress into animosity and dislike.

Do you see the same principle at work? Do you see that life is constantly changing? Do you understand that the currents which carry your thoughts are chemical reactions of molecules, strands, and spirals? It is these chemical reactions which are set into motion by your feelings and your moods. The only way to control your moods and feelings is by your thoughts. **What you think, is what you will become. What you fill your mind with, is what will fill your life.**

The Parent-Child Relationship

God is Pure Love, and as Pure Love He is in every cell and in every chemical reaction in the universe, but God also is very personal. He so loves His creation that He made you in His Love. He is with you in every action of your body, mind and heart.

Someone captured this idea in a song of your time. One which says, "Love makes the world go 'round."

This is a truth! Love makes everything go! Love is God in every action and reaction of life. Since love is spiritual, it is hard to identify or to see. You can only see the effects and not the actual love.

When you are a babe, you love because you are at that time producing an enormous amount of chemical reactions as you grow. Babies naturally love everything they see. But if a child is born into a home without love, and is not given love, he will slow the rate of chemical reactions and growth. Now do you understand why a child who is loved unconditionally grows in stature and in knowledge? Do you see that to guide a child, it is best done in love? Love is in every cell, and a child recognizes sincere love with every breath.

Be insincere with a child and you teach him to distrust. Punish a child too harshly and you teach him to hate. Distrust, hostility, and antagonism are the beginnings of hate. It is much easier to lead a child in love. Praise is better than condemnation. Praise a child's good points and attributes loudly. Criticize and you lose a child's interest and faith.

I have now entered into the parent-child relationship. The parent-child relationship is the easiest to heal with love. For the small child is chemically active and is surrounded by much love. When you give this child love, he recognizes it and is eager to have more love around him. He will gladly please you in every way.

But a precaution to parents: **teach a child to please God first, then himself, and later others.** Teach your child the correct line of communication. The first line of communication is with God, your higher self or spirit-self, and then others.

This parent-child relationship is so important, especially at this time. These children which are being taught now, are the future leaders of the new age and the new world. They will give your love, understanding and knowledge to the future generations of the new age. Have these lines of communication taught daily to the young. See to it that they understand the importance of love, appreciation and God.

Prayer

This information of love and all its properties is to demonstrate to each of you that there is more to God than you have opened your mind to. God is Love and, as this essence, His power is in every cell and action of your body. His Love is in your entire life: physical, emotional, mental and especially spiritual.

My desire is for you on earth to be informed. To know that you are facing some hard times, but within you, in every part of you, is God. He is always with you and available, as long as it is for the good of the whole.

Take this information to heart and consider truly what this means to you. You can never be apart from God. **It takes but a thought to activate the Power of God.** That is why, in times of trouble, you are moved to do something, either fight or run. There is an ability to act. In the future when the Earth trembles and moves, you will find that you must rely on an inner power to help you.

I ask each of you to prepare for anything and everything through prayer. As you already know, *prayer* is talking to God. *Meditation* is listening to God. By communing and talking to God you are revealing to Him nothing. He knows everything about you already, but in talking to God, you have opened the lines of communication to a very real presence inside you and in everything. This is where to look for your help, not in an outer building or in another person.

Your help comes from the ability to hear and talk to God inside your heart and mind. This very real Essence and Power is available to each of you, anytime, anyplace, and in all circumstances. You do not have to face a certain direction to talk to God. You do not have to enter a church building to commune with God. There are no special prayers or chants in order to communicate with God. He is in you and all around you. Say your prayers in your mind, enter the closet of your mind and talk to Him. **Learn to listen with your heart and mind. It is through the heart and mind that your answers will come.**

In the times ahead, you will be hard pressed to find someone to help you, as all people will be more concerned with their own survival. God will lead you; He will help you. **There is one requirement—you must ask God for the help; you must be able to hear His answer.** You must learn to be pliable and easily led from your own inner direction. These are mental attitudes, yet these are abilities which even the animals have. You are so much more than the animals. God is looking for you to survive by asking for His help.

You each hold the key to your survival, but **your spiritual survival is of the utmost importance.** Begin now to pray and to ask God to give you the understanding to comprehend. Some people are afraid to ask God for anything; their fear interferes in the prayer. You have built up such a fear of the Almighty, you expect Him to punish you. This is not how God works. His way is not one of punishment but of love. To overcome the fear of God, talk to Jesus Christ, His son, and ask for his help. The Christ consciousness is also in your mind, and can act as a bridge to God-Mind. Jesus Christ also sent the Holy Spirit to help you. All these beings are available to you for assistance, and aid of any kind.

Begin this day to pray. Prepare in this method for your future. Through prayer each will be prepared to face whatever is before him. The benefit is great. Every person who prays will grow and survive physically, emotionally, mentally, and most important, spiritually. Your spiritual growth is your real growth. For what you have in your soul is what is real. **What is carried in your mind is with you for all time, in all dimensions and in every plane.** The mental capacity to gain spiritual strength is tremendous. It is through the mind that God will guide you. That is how to commune with Him.

Listen in meditation for your guidance from God. The art of listening to God has been lost. Many people think they have the answers and are not in need of this guidance. Soon you will see, there will not be any place or person to help you. It will be **God speaking through your mind in your thoughts** that will give you direction. Every person's life depends on his ability to pray and listen to God.

5

A Message to Every Family

I have a message for every family in the world.

I T IS THROUGH YOUR RELATIONSHIPS with each other that many lessons are learned in this life. In this day and time on earth the family unit is all-important. My love is with the inner workings of families and the interrelationships in the family. I see the anguish which can affect the family. I hear through your prayers the concerns of the family, however loosely united they are. This is my message.

The first obligation of each individual in the family is to love, support and pray for each other. True, you are only responsible for your own actions, but through prayer and meditation the family unit is strengthened and made whole. All have congregated into each family unit to grow, live and learn together. There are no accidents of birth. As always, and in all things, this is your individual choice. You choose the family with which to unite.

The you who chooses the family is your entire self—the higher self and all personalities. The family situation is carefully selected with your life goals in mind. These parents, brothers and sisters have been of your choosing. You are united with this family for a cause and a purpose. The seeking of this cause and purpose is your goal. In finding the purpose you will find God. Your connection to His Great Mind will guide you in all decisions and lead in the paths of Truth.

Love holds the family together. Love can replace hostility and anger which simply cause you to alienate yourself from your good, which is only in God. Bring love back into the family by loving your spouse, parents, children, brothers and sisters. This love needs to be unconditional, as is the Love of God. **You do not need to approve of each other's actions in order to love.**

This love, which is a healing balm to the family unit, will be unconditional love. As individuals in the family unit are healed in love, so will cities, nations, planets and the entire universe be healed. This healing is ever-growing and ever-encircling as each individual pools his love. Release the Love of God into your family, cities, nations and into each individual who resides in your world.

Begin with yourself and your family unit. Love will not be contained in one small group. Love is ever-increasing and ever-moving in an outward search for more to love. Love is engulfing in its approach to mankind, but love must have a vehicle to be able to reach out to others. Become a vehicle of God's Love. Divine Love reaches out to the family, nation and world.

Here is how to bring the Love of God into your family: begin by prayer for yourself and your family to clear all angers, hostilities and fears from within. **Ask God to help you open your mind and heart each day to receive His Love, to allow His Love to pour through to your family.**

In meditation seek to bring the Love of God into your heart. See this Great Love beaming into your home. This is a mental exercise, but the mind and heart are your only method to reach God. This we have said over and over. Jesus repeated this same message in many different stories and in many different ways. I bring you the truth which was first given to

Abraham and to others throughout the world in different languages and in different cultures.

This is the same old story. It is imperative now for each person to find his connection to God and to grow spiritually, because this era is short of time. As this era comes to a close, there will be many who will lose their physical lives and will have wasted this precious time.

It is easier to work with God's Truth on earth, to practice and to prove these truths on earth. In the spiritual world all is accomplished through the mind. There is no hard, physical evidence of what you think. On earth your thoughts and attitudes are virtually turned into stone and matter. What you think is how you live. Your beliefs are the circumstances of your life. Do you consider yourself unworthy? The evidence of this belief is visible.

Take this precious time to prove God's Great Love to yourself and to your family. Bring more people into the circle of God's Love. Convert to your original essence in God, return, and prove to yourself what is worthy, what is true. This is only accomplished in prayer and meditation. Turn to God in your heart and mind. Return to God; He is the Love which is encircling this entire universe. Allow Him to enter your mind and heart. **It is your decision and choice to live in God's Love or to live in fear.**

Marriage

My call is to the whole world and I am telling you of events which will be monstrous and gigantic in scope. Not only are you to pray for yourselves and the world, but become close to the ones you love.

I would like to give some advice to the young who are considering marriage or who are currently in a marriage.

Marriage dear children, is for a lifetime and it can be a good life or one of hell. Marriage, as everything, is up to you! Make the most of it. **It is the commitment of the spirit which is important** and not the legalities of earth, but in honoring the laws of your nation and culture, you honor the commitment.

When you are truly committed to each other, your every thought will be for the good of both. You will begin and always think in terms of the family. This family unit, which you have started, is a world of itself. It should become as a world where only that which is good for the whole can be contemplated. It is the family unit which needs to be nourished with love and attention.

To the Groom: you have become head of a household, and it is up to you to set the pace for this marriage and this family unit. Always consider that you are now plural and no longer alone. All your thoughts and considerations are for the family unit. Perhaps the family unit only consists of you and your wife. It still is a unit, and as a unit, it should always be considered. What is good for one, must also be good for the other. When you hurt or harm your mate, you are hurting and harming yourself. Nothing in life goes unnoticed. That which you would try to hide will struggle to come out into the open. Events which you would hide from your mate will become known sooner or later, and believe me, later is worse.

As head of the household and co-caretaker, take this responsibility seriously. Create a union with your wife which is loving and respectful. In conversations you will learn about each other, your likes, dislikes and ways of conducting yourselves in different situations. Take the time and consideration to plan with your mate how you will guide your life and children, as they arrive. Remember always to rely on God and His Great Love for all your needs. Not only material needs, but the emotional and mental needs of your family. **Use love to govern and to seek solutions to all problems.**

To the Bride: you have the heart of the home in your hands. You set the tone with which your home runs. Bring into your home the love which is in your heart. Include love in all you do in and around your home. Even inanimate objects take on a new look and a new song when they are cared for and abide in love. Consider that the love which is in your heart on your wedding day can, and should, continue throughout your married life. Respect your husband and consider his feelings as you would your own.

You also must think in terms of a family unit and what is best for the whole unit. **Do all you can to maintain a harmonious household—one in which there is understanding, love and comprehension of all who reside in your home.** Consider that your first obligation is to your mate. It is through unity in marriage that this home was created. **Raise your children to honor and respect themselves, their home, their parents, and most importantly God, Creator of All.**

To the couple, old or young, renew the love daily by being thankful to God for your mate, marriage and home. Love is the feeling with which you talk to your mate or think of your mate. Love is how you care for your mate. Perhaps it is hard to be demonstrative and show your love. But there are always thoughts which can be sent to your love daily. There are small things which will show your love: a kind reply, a quiet pat on the arm, a vote of confidence, a please or thank you. These are the small things which make marriage a blessing instead of a curse.

Take serious thought of your partner and view this person as he or she truly is. Everyone will have faults. The reason we are on earth is to correct these faults. No one person is perfect and no one marriage is perfect. To expect perfection is not reality. To expect your partner not to become angry, depressed or ill is unrealistic. These are the times when you most need to show your love.

Through all kinds of living: happiness and sadness, illness and health, feast and famine, you are married, not simply in a story book type of life. **Married life requires each to become totally unselfish.** Always think of your mate and the rest of the family unit. All decisions are to be made with this in mind.

Learn to be dependable and trustworthy. It will take these qualities to have a good marriage. This is a true partnership. Always have the inclusion of your partner in all decisions not out of fear, but out of love. Seek to hear and listen to your partner's words, listen with your ears, heart and mind. Come to know, understand and respect your partner. In this way you will truly be one. It takes effort, but it is well worth it. Nothing can compare to a happy and contented home life. Praise what you have in a partner, see the good qualities, the good points of this person. There had to be good qualities and points, or you would not have married this person in the first place!

Build on the good and set aside fear, hate, hostility and anger. These emotions bring ruin and destruction to any relationship.

In the coming years it will take strong marriages and strong partnerships for the family, such an important part of God's plan, to survive. Joseph and I had a wonderful marriage in which we were happy most of the time. But we were very human while on earth. We know the problems which can arise in a marriage. Today you have many more interferences and distractions.

We admire your integrity, ambition and persistence in trying to make marriage a part of your world. This is very difficult in today's time, but it is not impossible. With God's help your marriage can be beautiful. Strengthen your marriage and partnerships. You will need the love and comfort which can only be found in a home. It will be difficult to survive the coming events without the love and support of the family.

Do not bring children into this world unless you can commit a huge amount of work and love to these individuals. Bring children into a home in which there is love and under-

standing. The little children born at this time have much to face
in their future. True, this is the choice they made in spirit. But
help the little ones with guidance and care. This will set them
in the right direction.

Marriage will become the important part of your lives
once again. Marriage will give you the refuge from the outer
world and a haven to rest in. This is how each marriage should
be. Spirit requires this union of male and female. Even in
today's world, where you have such an easy time ridding
yourselves of mates, you still seek to unite with another.

**It takes commitment on the part of the male and female
to make a marriage what it can be.** If only one makes the
commitment it will not work, for it will take both individuals
working, loving and seeking the same general goals as a family
unit.

Familial Love

Today the young speak much of love, but do not live love.
The young romanticize love and think of love as some wonderful cure-for-all. Love is seen as magical in quality. Pure Love,
which is God, is magical and a cure-for-all. Human love has not
reached these heights. People confuse Divine Love with romantic love. In some languages there are different terms for these
kinds of love. But your language is lacking in terms and con-
glomerates all kinds of love into one general term.

Romantic love is a glimpse of Divine Love. It is but a
preview of Divine Love. Romantic love, which so envelopes the
young, is only the illusion of Divine Love. If you are constantly
looking for romantic love you will be going from partner to
partner and from mate to mate. **Divine Love is something
which is obtained only in and through the spiritual realm.**
This type of love, romantic love, is not practical in a marriage
and you must be practical. Romantic love lacks the substance
of Divine Love.

Now general love is called esteem, caring and admiring in other languages. It is general love you feel for all life forms: for your pet, friend, neighbors and countrymen. This is a good element of love and one which needs to be a part of your marriage. As you love all life, general love will grow.

Within the family unit is a love which I will call, for want of a better term, familial love. This is the type of love which will unite your family in love and purpose. This is the love which grows to include all members of the family unit. The love which you and your mate have will be an incorporation of all these loves.

It would behoove you to ask God to fill your home with Divine Love. This is the love which will heal the arguments and the unpleasantries of learning to live in intimacy. Divine Love will become the substance of your marriage.

The Children

As a child it is easy to live in a family, for at first you are not responsible for much of anything except to smile at mommy and daddy and be cute. Then, if you are in the right family, your every endeavor is seen as new and exciting. This is how you grow in confidence and understanding. But dear ones, these were the days of your childhood; they have passed. As you grow, your responsibilities should grow also.

It is good to teach the children how to behave, what is expected of them from the culture in which your family finds itself. There are stories to tell, of your nation, people and family. These stories must be passed on to the young, to be given to their young. As a child reaches the age of majority, he will act differently and be expected to conduct himself in a manner appropriate for a mature adult in his culture. It is important to put aside the childish ways and childish thoughts of "me first."

Now in your culture, the young make their own marital choices. I see the error of this in that you, as a nation, have not taught your young to be responsible. Therefore, they have no maturity or wisdom in making a decision which should be made for life. I would caution you as parents in this nation, and in this time, to shape this child into an adult capable of caring for himself. The crime and drug use of the world today are an escape from reality. It is the responsibility of the home to give this knowledge.

Far too long the family has been left to fate. This is not where the family should be. In most cases, this generation has not had the reality of a stable home. I see the pockets of homes formed in stability and in true love, but these are few and they cannot undo the ignorance and unwillingness of the rest.

The young of this generation will be needed to make a difference. It is up to this generation to find the way to lead, to prepare their young to face a harsh future—one which will be completely different from today's world. It will be up to the family unit to educate its younger family members in the spiritual, cultural and national lessons which will impart knowledge and wisdom.

Now I speak to those of you who have already chosen your mate. Love this individual! Care for this individual as all humans on earth should be cared for; continue to love this mate and see the good qualities in this person. You have chosen this person for good reasons. Magnify the good and see your love for this person grow. Make a commitment together to form a united family—one which will see the good in each person and magnify that good. You always have the Spiritual Creative Being to instill His Love into your family.

Once the commitment has been made, honor it. Bring the following elements into your family unit: humor, joy, love, understanding, compassion, kindness, respect for each individual and peace. Continue with this general attitude. Think of your mate in these terms, and it will be easier to have the good marriage you desire in your inner being.

To the young who are contemplating marriage or in the process of choosing a mate, I say look past romantic love. First see a friend, and then a lover. Take a good look at your choice for maturity and respect of oneself. This is important. Put away the rose-colored glasses of romance and see the reality of this person. Seek those qualities which tell if the individual is mature. It will take maturity to live together, to start a family united. Do not confuse age with maturity. Maturity of character is what to look for. Consider this a life commitment and see it as one which is irrevocable. This will demonstrate to you the seriousness of choosing a life partner.

Bless your family unit in spirit and in love. Pray. Ask God to enter your heart and mind, to bring into your home a new understanding and love. Through prayer, errors can be rectified. God can make a new person of you, and then family members will have to treat you differently.

Abuse

Now a word of caution: I see the abuse of people, especially in the home. Abuse is not in God's favor. He would not have one of you live one day with abuse. If you find yourself with an abusive partner, leave. Do not come near this abusive person until he or she is truly healed of their abusive nature. Abuse is one of the elements in the world today which is destructive and will destroy the family unit. The family cannot be united in abuse, only in love. Through prayer, ask God to heal the abuser and the abused. This cycle of abuse must stop, and it can only stop in the family which becomes united in God's Love.

A United Family

Allow me to give an example of a united family. It is one in which the parents view each other with respect, with love and with their commitment firm in their minds. As each child is born into this model family, he or she is received in love and seen as an individual. The child has been placed in this family to honor and love. Teach the child the ways of your people, and forms of conduct which will allow it to live life in love and peace. When a dispute arises, do not allow anger to escalate into violence or abusive words. After the emotions have quieted, the problem can be viewed. Always keep the good of the whole family unit in mind. Both partners should have their say, be heard and acknowledged for their opinion.

Prayer and meditation will bring the uniting of the family. God will set into your minds how to solve every problem. Prayer is very important, for God should be the One who is sought for the settling of all disputes. The family which brings into its midst the Creative Spirit of the Universe is bringing into the family All-Good and All-Love.

Pray not only for yourself, but for your life partner. **I ask that God's Divine Love be brought into each family in the world. Pray for your family each night and day, and remember all families in the world.** It will be the families which have learned to rely on God who will be able to weather the storms. It will be the united family who will be able, in love, to correct and lead the children of the future. The united family will care for its old and hear the wisdom they have to give. Each member of the family will be respected, loved and honored. This is what I see missing in today's families on earth.

Training the Young

Joseph and I gave Jesus the family where he first learned of God's Love and Wisdom. Our home was not one of luxury or misery. We had plenty of food, and a nice, comfortable place to raise our children. We sang to them and taught them the ways of our culture and our religion. We also taught each that God is alive, and willing to help them live their lives to the fullest.

God will not impose Himself on any of His children. **It is up to each individual to ask God to enter into a union with him.** First, earnestly seek to find God in your heart and mind. Become united fully with The Creator of this world and universe. You will see God at work in your spouse and children. This is the easiest and best way to be united, as a family.

In our home, we taught Jesus and his brothers to **honor work, food, nature and all creation.** God was very much a part of our lives and of our home. There was laughter and there were tears. As the children grew, we included them in the decisions of the family in order that they might learn to run a family of their own. The children were always told the truth in every situation. The girls were taught to be good mothers and wives. They were given, as was the custom of our day, instruction in the duties which corresponded to them as females.

But they also learned to use their individual talents to earn a living, if the need should arise. This also gave their creative nature an outlet. It taught them to take their creativity as a means of support, as life is not a certainty. We taught them that this life on earth was for a little while. Each member of the family was to develop his or her talent because it was God-given, and use it to bring in extra money for himself.

Now as each earned his money, he was taught to give the first part to God, as a way of thanking God for the talent in the first place. Then a part was given to the family unit for the good of the whole, and the rest was his to keep or spend.

They were also taught to save, to put aside some for another day, not much, but a sample of their work. This they could use for supplies to make more use of their talents or to keep as a reward for work done well.

Now in this day, I see parents being more concerned with their children's pleasures than with their ability to seek God. You must learn what is important and what is not important. First is the ability to rely and trust in God's Love to lead you. The family should be viewed as a whole unit; nothing should be done to lessen the whole. When the children are exalted above the parents, there is unbalance. When the parents set themselves up as dictators, this is also unbalanced. The family as a whole should benefit and each person should have the opportunity to learn to find God in his heart and mind. This is the responsibility of the home and family.

Seek God first, then all things will be added to you as an individual and as a family.

See the Planet as One Family Unit

The family is a microcosm of the world. We are all one family. We each need to be treated with respect, love and honor. **Begin to see the world as your family.** Every soul on this planet is a creation of the One Great Creator. Every culture is honorable, every race is to be honored as God's creation, every nation is a brother, every religion is a sister. Look to the sameness of life on this planet. See that the same love is expressed in every member of every nation.

Children of the Planet Earth, care for your home, which is this planet. Care also for your brothers, sisters, parents, and grandparents. All are members of the family of Earth. There is only one Creator, One Great Spirit whose life flows through every person, plant, animal and rock of this planet. Consider the Planet Earth as a whole family of the Great Creator.

View the whole world as family members and see the planet as one unit. These divisions amongst yourselves are destructive. This is holding you on earth back from uniting. Become members of the Planet Earth and not different nations.

In order to become universal, it will be necessary for you to break these old habits of division and derision. The whole Planet Earth is one family unit and all people should be considered as one unit. These ways of dividing are hindering your progress in the universal world. **Until you on earth can stop the wars, you are not ready to join the family of the universe.**

When the time comes that the world can be seen as one family unit, there will be peace. Begin now to let this idea grow in your mind. We will consider each nation as a family and each religion as a family, but all related by the life-force which animates you individually. It is God's Life which is flowing in each body. **We are all united by this One Creative Being who created not only me, but each individual soul who has ever lived on this earth.**

The Sameness of All Creation

In the world, we are all as different as the flowers which grow across the lands. We each bring our own beauty to this family-world. Each nation, each culture, brings the beauty and richness of its past, the individual uniqueness of its identity. As the colors of your skin interweave in this great family crest, it is beautiful.

Put aside your anger and allow each culture and each nation to teach the other. Allow each religion to teach the other and take into consideration that we all are giving our gratitude to the One Creator of the Universe. It matters not what you call our Creator. It matters not how you worship our Creator. All that matters, and is important, is that each person be thankful for the life which flows through him, that each respects the life-force which animates us all.

Look at the individual nations and religions. See the differences? Now begin to note the sameness. **We were not created by different Creators.** This world was not created by different beings, but by one Great Spirit who is, at this moment, flowing through the rocks, trees and through each of you as you breathe. Look not to the differences, but allow me to point out the sameness of each person.

Each individual, male or female, is constructed in the same manner. Every person in this world is made of skin, bone, cells, tissue, blood, of the same components. Take a sample of each race of man, in the cell and in the tissue of each organ, the heart, kidney, liver, lungs, bone, muscle, brain, blood, etc. Each is constructed exactly alike. Not somewhat alike, but exactly alike. One race could not be distinguished from the other without the skin color. Each female and male conceive their young in the same manner. Each child is born into this world in the same manner. Every individual has the same feelings, the same methods of thinking. Does one think with his lungs and another with his kidneys? No, all think with the functioning of their brains and every heart beats exactly alike.

Every individual child born on this earth requires the same care in order to survive. Each child needs to be fed, clothed and cared for. Each child needs to be taught the same. Each nation has its own history and manner of conducting itself. It is not too different from other nations. Do not look to the differences. See how all people need to be loved and to love, all need to eat daily and have water. All people of the world have a need to work. Every person has the same basic needs.

Each religion is worshiping, underneath the outer trappings, its Creator. **It is the same Creator!** Whether you pray facing the east or facing an altar, or on Saturday or Sunday, it is all worship. You each are grateful to the Creator, no matter what you call Him. The dogma and the rituals are not as important as the worship which is done in your heart and mind.

Allow us to view the world as a whole and each nation, each religion as part of this Great Whole. **Be tolerant, one of the other.** All religions are man-made, inspired by the Creator. All words which have been written in the Holy Books have been written by men in unity with the Creator. The only place for you as individuals to worship, and to have communion with your Creator, is in your mind and in your heart.

I do not condone abuse of any kind, whether it is abuse of one nation against another, or abuse of one individual against another. I will not condone abuse of one religion against another. Taking up arms and fighting for your religion and your dogma is wrong, abusive and ugly. It is not pleasing to your Creator. He made you and this world in love. It is in love He desires you to live. There is no chosen people or special chosen church. There are many chosen people and many churches. It is for each person to choose how he will worship his Creator.

Humans, earthlings, you are many, but there is only One Creator. **You are as cells in the Creator's body.** Think in terms of big, huge, and gigantic when you think of your Creator. It matters not what you call Him. It is the calling on Him in your mind and hearts that matters. One color of skin is not better than the other. All were created alike. There is no one supreme race of men, all are the supreme people and all are the chosen ones.

Each religion is guilty of interpreting its Holy Writings to indicate the message the interpreter wants to make. Any religion is correct if it leads you to worship the Creator through your heart and mind. **It is through your mind and heart that true prayers are said.** The religious and cultural differences are outer. Look to the inner longings and desires of the heart; there you will see the same emotions, longings and ambitions. These are what you are to look for in your brother and sister. The world is a family, the world is one unit in the universe.

Your home is the Planet Earth. Why do you bomb her and destroy her oceans with waste? Why do you destroy her

forest and her seacoast? This is your home. Take care of her. This is the only home you have to leave to your children.

Is this the care and the appreciation you are showing your Creator? He provided you with all the elements to continue this world. It is you who are destroying Earth, it is you who are destroying yourselves.

Love, care and respect are the answer. Honor the Creator by honoring His Creation. Respect the Creator by respecting every insect, pebble and grain of sand. Honor the air you breathe, the forest and the sea. Care for this world and its inhabitants, each animal and each person. Smile and sing the song of life. Send thoughts of love throughout the atmosphere and surround this planet in your love. This is how to begin to heal her wounds.

Only through love will the coming earth changes be met. With honor and respect the coming changes, which will be huge and gigantic in scope, will be faced. Know that there is a better way to raise your young and to view your world. It will be a new family of earthlings, a new land, a new city and a new day.

Begin now in your mind and in your heart. This very minute make a commitment to honor. Respect each nation, each religion and put aside your warring thoughts. Send out love, honor and respect to every individual on earth. Talk to the planet. Tell every tree you are grateful for its shade and beauty.

Honor your home in the same way. Talk to the chair you sit in; thank it for allowing you a place to sit. Be grateful to your bed for the comfort and rest it gives. Tell your mate of your love, honor and respect for him or her. Tell your home of the gratitude and the comfort which you receive in her walls. It is not after the earth changes that you are to begin, but now, this moment, this very instant.

It is now time to begin to truly worship God, your Creator. Now is the time to set up the lines of communication to your Maker. Now, before the turmoil. Now before you desperately need His counsel. **Begin now to rely upon and love your Creator.** Feel Him stirring in your heart.

Now my dear family, learn these lessons well. Follow these teachings I give you. Put them in your minds and hearts. Practice what you learn daily. Most important, set up the lines of communication to God. He is waiting for your invitation to enter and be a part of your life. His Love will smooth the rough places, the angers and hurts. Allow His Love to flow through your heart, mind and home. Bring God into every part of your life: your marriage, job, obligations and your every purchase. This is how to live totally in God's presence.

6

Mary's Message to the World

Today I wish to speak to the hearts and minds of all men, women, and children.

PREPARE ON EARTH to have a long life in spirit. Here all is accomplished with your minds. It takes training in how to use your mind. Every thought is seen by all. There is no place to hide in spirit.

Begin this training on earth by first asking God to strengthen your faith in Him. Listen to all your own thoughts and hear what is coming into your mind. There is much in your heart and mind which needs to be eliminated. Would you like to have these thoughts viewed by all? The only way to cleanse your mind and heart is through prayer and meditation. It will be to your advantage to do this quickly.

Your time on earth is short, for by the turn of this century many of you will be here in spirit but not on earth. Many catastrophes will occur in the latter part of this century. Many will lose their lives on earth. The opportunity to return to life on earth will be diminished for many, many years. Some will live in this spiritual realm for hundreds of years. Now is the time to find God in your heart and mind. Now is the time to prepare for your return to this spiritual realm. This can only be accomplished in prayer and in meditation, which connects you to your Creator.

God is a God of Love! It is His will that none should waste his or her life in idle pursuit of earthly pleasures which do not have merit in spirit. **He has allowed me the opportunity to appear in many places and to bring this message to every man, woman and child on earth today.** This is your opportunity to find peace and love as it is only found in God.

Pray first for your soul, then your loved ones, then for each person on earth today. This is true communion with God. It does not matter what your religious affiliation is. There is only One God, who is Creator of All. In different parts of the world He is known by different names. In different religions He is known by different names. Call Him THE LORD GOD CREATOR OF ALL. The name which you use to address this Creator is not important. The important fact is that you desire to contact Him and to connect to His Spirit.

These wars which are now being fought because of religious differences do not please God. The wars which you fight for political reasons do not please God. You are as small children who have not learned to allow others freedom of opinion. You have not taken the example of your Creator, who allows freedom of choice in all matters.

I am also known in different parts of the world by different names, and to all I will be appearing. I call to all nations for your true conversion. **This word "conversion" simply means returning to the original. Your original beginning was God, who created you in His image.**

Yes, I have given this message to others. I have appeared in many parts of the world already. And I am now appearing to the six children of Yugoslavia. This is the message which I have given them. Three words are the main points:

Conversion—A return to your original beginnings, to God.

Peace—For all men, women, and children on earth today. Stop the fighting and the wars. Put aside the use of all pollutants, chemicals which harm life and drugs which harm your minds. Your mind is your only connection with the spiritual realm and with God, the Creator of All.

Prayer—Through prayer you come to the very Presence of your Creator, God. Take the word "prayer" and give it its true meaning: conversing with God, the Creator. Talk to God in your mind as you talk to your mother, wife, brother or sister. HE is all of these to you and much, much more. HE is Love, Understanding and All Knowledge. Bring all your problems and your concerns to Him today and now. Pray for your world, planet and your own life which is spiritual.

I will continue to appear in many different parts of the world. Some appearances you will hear of, some you will not, but in every place I will make a sign, give proof of my existence and my concern. In many instances there will be places of healing left to prove my point. In others, there will be visual demonstrations. In some there will be both. **I come to you through this method to speak quietly with you and to ask for your prayers for this world, the planet Earth.**

This person taking this dictation was chosen by me, by the Holy Spirit and by God Himself to bring this message of Hope and of True Conversion. She was chosen because she was not looking for acknowledgment of any kind. Through her desire to be in contact with God, she sought to know and hear the truth of her being. She looked for God, through much prayer and much meditation. It is not the length of time which is spent in prayer and meditation but the earnestness of your seeking. It is the truth of your desire which gains you favor. It is your consistent attitude of prayer and gratitude for all you have in this beautiful world.

I would so like for all men to return to their original selves and to comprehend their own natures, which are Divine. Tell the people of this world that unless they repent in their hearts and souls of their selfish ways, they will lose lifetimes of spiritual growth. Each individual can do his part to bring peace and love to this earth.

You will not be "punished" by the turning of the globe. You simply will not have the opportunity to set into practice your goals. Every individual came to this earth with a life plan, goals which the soul set for itself. Today most of these souls have lost sight of their plans and have been caught up in the vices of the world. These vices are insidious, for they rob the person of his ability to seek God. The people who use drugs are wasting this lifetime in idle pleasure. Vices can be anything which take you away from your Divine goal and search. There are those who look to drugs, violent and pornographic movies, sexual deviations, and games, whether to gamble or simply watch.

The TV is one of the biggest distractions for man today. Someone else is controlling your brain for that time period.

Some people give themselves totally to their careers and work. When this becomes the entire focus of a life, then it is an obsession and is wrong.

Every person alive feels the need to help others. This is because deep inside us we know that, as one progresses, all progress. As each individual reaches higher levels of thinking and of ideals, then the whole world is aided. That is why everyone likes to help. Universally the need to help is great. The will to be heroic is in everyone. There are no heros, for when you help another, you help yourself.

It is only as a whole unit that mankind can advance. Soon a giant leap into the future will occur. Those who are not mentally prepared will be at a loss to understand or comprehend. This is growth! It will be a bigger universe which you will occupy in the future. The Earth will be renewed in field, forest and in all kingdoms. The survival of the fittest is a truth. But we do not talk only of physical fitness, but of mental and spiritual fitness.

A wonderful and bright future is at hand. A wonderful new tomorrow will arrive. Think in terms of this wonderful event. Put out of your mind thoughts of negativity and doom. What will transpire is glorious and splendid.

This land of America began as a country founded on Truth and good principles, but over the years much corruption has taken its toll on the citizens of the world. Many countries are now being led by self-centered and self-serving men. You have forgotten the ways of your ancestors and as a country have forgotten why this nation came into existence. Your country, as all other countries of this world, are regulated and ruled by just a few powerful men who are looking out for their own interests. The world problems have become too complex and too large to be handled.

What is needed on earth today, is that each individual alive on this planet brings his heart and mind to the One God to be cleansed and to be renewed. As each individual becomes centered in the Truth of the One God and in His guidance, all beings on earth will be safer and better prepared to continue to live their life wherever they find themselves. Not all people will survive these changes with their physical life intact. But all will continue to live in spirit.

There is always growth and progress in the universe and in each individual. Sometimes it seems that we take one step forward and two steps back, but we are nevertheless progressing. Nothing on earth or in the universe is static; nothing continues unchanged. Always there is change, and this change brings more good than can be seen.

The Universe is Expanding

Lift up your mind and heart to those thoughts which will be gratifying to all people. Lift up your thoughts to consider other levels of existence of which you know not. Lift up your thoughts so that all that is seen is good.

The universe is growing and expanding. The truth is that all things grow and this growth is causing your Earth to turn, but as with everything, there is always more than one cause. And in this case there are many causes.

For one, it is time for this rotation of land and sea to take place. Another reason is that your civilization is polluting this planet. For another, not only is this planet becoming polluted, but the minds and hearts of the young are stunted by the use of drugs. Also, there is much corruption in the leaders of the different countries.

There is now a break-down of all values and standards. These standards are what caused your forefathers to settle in this new land and to seek their own freedom to worship God in their own way. Now this country has come full circle and is trying to place its standards on the world. There is no need for any one country to believe it has all the answers for the world. **Only God has the right answers for you on earth.**

The rumblings of the Earth now are causing your scientists to wonder what is happening. They are dragging their feet in releasing the information they have acquired. These men of science have been observing for many months and for many years the evolution of the solar system. They do not know what to think of these changes. They do not have any records of such events and they do not want to go out on a limb. So instead, they watch and transcribe the changes and speculate on the meaning.

Our mission is to warn and alert the common man of the coming catastrophic events.

I will change the places of my apparitions and be appearing to the people of South America. They are deep in the trade of drugs. They know the consequences and dangers of these leaves. The drug trade is not only wiping the truth from the minds of the young, but is also robbing the world's economy. The ability of a few men to rule through fear and the use of drugs is wrong, and not at all pleasing to God.

Now is the time for repentance and for the transforming of your life on earth. Now is the time of returning to the basic lessons of olden days.

The planet is a living organism and is also a part of a larger and alive universe. Since this planet is also imbued with the Life Force, which is the essence of God, it is never stagnant, but growing in all ways. There are many new developments in store for earthlings and those who reside on other planets. Now is a time for a realigning of the spiritual self with the Whole of Spirit.

Now is the time for all minds to open and allow God to gain entrance. This is the only salvation of spiritual growth. All growth is mandated by God and is set into motion by God. Therefore the growth of this great universe is now blossoming into a new and more wonderful whole.

The planet Earth is in dire danger and all its inhabitants are also in this peril. The wars, chemical use on the soil and in the minds of men is destroying your planet.

The warnings and pleas I wish to give to all who reside on this planet are for a return to the Truth—the Truth of God, which is that God is the Creator of All, and it is by His Power that the universe is in existence.

The truth is that man must spend much time in prayer and meditation. Too much emphasis is placed on worldly affairs and on worldly issues. You who live on earth today are much as those souls who inhabited Sodom and Gomorrah. It is only your own pleasure which interests you. It does not matter who is hurt and suffers, in order for man to have the pleasures of the flesh. The accumulation of worldly goods is in vain, for these things will not endure the test of time. Only your soul endures the test of time. Only in your heart and mind can you find truth and happiness.

Leave the gossip and the turmoil behind you. Leave aside all thoughts and conditions which distress. Put away your need to control and dominate. Set aside your bad and negative thoughts. Get rid of hate, fear and lust. These are not conditions befitting a child of the One True God. Return to your original premise—to the starting place of all life. Return to God by prayer and meditation.

My desire is that every being on earth spends one hour daily in prayer and in meditation. This I would consider a minimum. Only by this means can your species be saved. Only by this kind of commitment will your planet be saved from destruction. Pray for the land, seas, heavens and the people. Say prayers for peace and understanding to come into the minds of the leaders of all nations. Pray for the young who will survive the tilting of the Earth. And pray for the old who will most likely not survive. Pray for a new beginning, a new land, a new heaven and a new species of man.

I would have all people spend a daily time in prayer. **True prayer is the ability to talk simply with God.**

I wish to explain how everyone is to contact God. It is one thing for me or someone else to say, "Talk to God in your heart and in your mind." It is another for you on earth to understand the meaning of these words. Most people do not realize that they talk to themselves all the time. Your minds are very active and always mulling over some subject. Usually it is worry which preoccupies you.

Let us consider worry. When you worry, you use your mind to dream up images of the worst possible kind. Is this not so? Say a loved one is late in returning. Your mind begins to bring up pictures of accidents or deception, then at the same time your heart begins to beat faster and your hands become sweaty. Not only is your mind working overtime, but your feeling nature is also involved.

Let us turn this same experience into a prayer. A loved one is late; you become concerned. Imagine that you can call God on a telephone and you tell Him the loved one is late. You ask for His help. At this point in time, your feeling nature will find comfort and peace. Your heart will tell you all is being taken care of.

Is this not a more pleasant way to face the same situation? If you become so worried that you cannot calm yourself, then begin to repeat *The Lord's Prayer* or any other written prayer you know. These written prayers are a help to your subconscious mind, for the words themselves will calm your conscious mind and your feelings. When all else fails and you allow yourself to become desperate, you can simply call out to God for help. Help will be there instantly.

My desire and wish is that all people use every available minute to pray. Use any form of prayer which gives you comfort. Remember that there are as many ways to pray as there are people. **Each is a unique individual and each has his own way of praying.**

In the next few years, as the Earth begins to tremble and shake, it will give you comfort to have set up the lines of communication to God. You will already know how to pray and feel the presence of the One God. You on earth will need this to endure all the upheavals which will occur.

My message is being given to many people throughout the world. In many places I am appearing. My warnings are coming to the world by every available means. The world is turning a deaf ear to them. The news media will not report all my apparitions or give my messages as given. Much censoring of my words is occurring.

People are afraid to list all the disasters which will take place. They fear many things: looking like a fool, sounding a warning which is not true. For various and varied reasons my message has been censored in the past.

Now I wish every word which you receive from me be given to the world. Do not fear that these predictions will not occur. I would have had your world spared of these great calamities, but it is too late for that. The planet is in need of a renewing. The atmosphere is in need of a cleansing. The race consciousness needs to be cleansed. All we can do now is warn the people.

We also want the multitudes to prepare their hearts to come to the spirit world, for many will lose their physical lives, and many will be bewildered at that time. The confusion will be great. Many will have no idea where they are or what has happened.

Prepare your heart and mind to receive the very Spirit of God. Prepare to judge yourself and to make amends for your prejudices, intolerances, fears, jealousy, envy, animosity and false pride. These are the errors of the flesh. It will be your undoing not to forgive.

First, **you must forgive yourself.** Then forgive all others who have hurt you in the slightest.

Bring peace into your family and to your home. Allow this peace to flow out of your home into the world around you. Send thoughts of love to all people on earth. Do not allow countries, religions, or anything to keep you from sending out the Love of God. It is only by love and prayer that you will be safe. It is only by peaceful thoughts that the wars will end.

Be tolerant and kind to those who are different. Perhaps the differences are only in opinion, or perhaps in looks or color of skin, but none of these things matter. All that matters is to have the love and peace of God distributed throughout the world to all people.

Keep peace and love alive in your heart and in your home. Keep the song of peace and love in your heart. Keep the meaning of peace and love in your everyday experiences. My word for today is peace. My word for all time is peace. My warning for the world is peace. Look to each other and see only through the eyes of love, see only peace in each countenance.

It is true my wish is for peace to reign among men, that true conversion be among men, and for everybody to return to God. I wish all people to turn to God and look to their own God-Mind connection to see them through the coming earth changes.

The Church is aware of my predictions and still it withholds the information. It is the faithful whom I wish to reach. I speak now to the people who come from far away in hope of seeing me. **The repentance is of a spiritual nature. It is seeking to be one with your very God-Essence.** It is a return to your original beginnings. This is the conversion I wish you to find. It is not for my good, but for each of you to receive the full Spirit of God, to have true happiness which is only available to you in spirit.

True happiness is being one with God. True wealth is being united with God-Mind. All health and wholeness emanate from God. This is the only source of everything good.

I wish to bring this message, because in the near future there will be many disasters which will occur on earth. Much of the land will be moved and mountains will fall. The oceans will bubble and churn. There will be gigantic tidal waves which will wash away multitudes of people from the face of the Earth. In that time many will arrive in this spiritual realm in total confusion and for awhile there will be chaos. This I wish to avoid. If you on earth are better prepared to return to spirit, then this process will go smoothly.

My desire is not for lip-service to the Church or to the saints, but a true turning around of lives—a true transplantation of beliefs, a true opening of your mind and heart to the Spirit of God. The Earth is near the end of an era. The Earth will have a new look and a new feel. It is time for this renewal and it is time for this end. Only in an ending can there be a new beginning.

The new age will be upon you soon. But it will not come about without some pain. The new era needs to be born. And its birth is what will give rise to the calamities which will overtake the Earth.

My predictions will come as foretold. I have been given the commission to warn and to send out this alarm of the coming danger. By every means I am imploring each person alive on earth today to think and to feel the truth of these words.

For years I have been giving this warning and soon it will all start to transpire. In the future I will tell of the glorious times in the new age and new era. It will be wonderful and peaceful.

But for now I wish to have as many as will listen to my voice in their hearts, heed this warning. Contemplate the message: return to God, seek to know more of your Creator, restore your faith in Truth.

It is imperative that the world join together at this time to pray to God. Prayer will be easy, for everyone worships the One God, however He is called by different names in different parts of the world.

My plea is for all people of the world to turn to whatever concept of God is in their hearts: to begin with this concept and allow God to fill their beings with a sense of peace and safety. My desire is that all people return to their spiritual lessons of old; to begin where they are and with whatever spiritual concept they have, reach out to the One God of the Universe who is Creator of All. As you turn to your Creator and pray as you know how, a peaceful, safe feeling will enter hearts and fill people to capacity with the very Spirit of God. It will take much prayer and meditation to bring about changes in the hearts of all men. It will take a committed effort on everyone's part to bring about the spiritual renewing that will make the changing of the Earth easier.

Seek not so much to heal your physical bodies as your spiritual natures. Seek to find God in your hearts and minds. Place your faith in The Almighty God of All. Trust the One God to bring spiritual healing to all who seek. Pray for peace on earth and among men.

I seek to embrace all people with my love. I wish to encircle all people on earth in a safety net which will save your souls. The soul is that innermost part of you which is connected to the Divine Being. Bring your prayers for peace, conversion, hope and prosperity to the altar of God which is in your mind. Seek the miracles which will occur in your life and in your loved ones' lives. Bring the names of these people to your altar and ask for the highest possible gift, a spiritual healing.

Put aside your mischievous nature and let go of all fear, envy, doubt, confusion and malice. Allow the true nature of God to permeate your very essence. This is the only way to bring about a brighter and more peaceful future for the next generations.

It matters not what religion you belong to, but it does matter what your spiritual values are. It also matters how much diligence you use to seek God. **The sincerity and attitude in your heart as you pray are important.** These are the issues which will give you peace and understanding. It is what is needed to bring this new age into the world. The new millennia is fast approaching. With the new century will come some dramatic changes all over the world.

Prepare yourself for this new era and for the changes by prayer and meditation.

My words must be heard, they must be listened to with your inner heart and your intellect. I speak the truth. In the near future you will have need for spiritual development.

The planet itself is crying out to God to save it from the destruction of man. You have decimated and destroyed the natural beauty, the ecology and the chain of renewal which this planet's life is dependent upon. You have wasted much of the land with chemicals which not only destroy the pests, but the very life from the dirt and the rocks. This chemical dependence has begun to infest all areas of life from the soil, to the insect, to each branch of life on earth.

The chemicals which are invading your bodies are doing harm not only to you but to your future generations. The water has been contaminated with chemicals. Your minds are being contaminated with drugs which are chemicals, and with non-use. Do you not see the danger which is apparent at every turn? Do you not see the harm which you are bestowing on the future of your children? Can you be so blind to the fact that when you destroy this planet, you have destroyed your own home?

How long will it be before you awaken to the damage and destruction which has taken place? How many of the animals must be destroyed for all future time before you see the danger to yourselves? There is corruption of the land and sea. What of the corruption of your spirit?

The soul, which is what lives forever, is also being destroyed by your attitudes and your dependence on drugs which inhibit your thinking capacity. How can you destroy all that God has made? How can you on earth be so heartless and unthinking? The future of your world is at stake. The future of your children is in your hands. The future of all time, is now.

The planet will eventually care for itself. It will destroy much life, but then you have destroyed much of Earth's life. The planet will bring itself back together at the cost of many lives. **Is your spiritual life prepared for a return to reality, the reality of spiritual values, and a spiritual way of life?** Men of earth, are you prepared to face the consequences of these actions?

Yes, I know this seems to be a punishment from God, but to the contrary, it is simply the effect of your actions on the planet. Many things are occurring at this time. This is an age of change. There is growth in the Universe. There is the effect of the destruction which man has caused to the planet. All these things together will cause many violent reactions on earth. Prepare for this world to change and for there to be great changes in your lifetime.

There is only one hope and that is God. There is only one life and that is God. There is only one way to save yourself and that is also in God.

My children, spend time in prayer and meditation. Use whatever method you have been taught. All prayer is good and all requests which come from a sincere heart are good. Do not try to deceive God for He knows every thought which abounds in this world. Nothing, absolutely nothing, bypasses Him. **Come with a sincere heart and an open mind, and ask God to prepare you for all events.**

People of Earth, hear my words, listen to this call, repent and return to your God, which is the One God of the Universe.

I have already explained that conversion is a return to the original, which is your true beginning. This true beginning is God. From God we all came and to God we all desire to return.

This word "repentance" is a returning to truth. Return to God and in returning you will have repentance. You cannot hold the idea of God and the idea of fear in your mind at the same time. When you are truly repentant of past mistakes you cannot at the same time hold on to any part of your mistaken thinking. To repent is to release all that keeps you from God. Let go of fear. Do not fear anything, not even the coming planetary changes. Release all feelings of hopelessness. Your hope is in God.

On earth you have been caught up in certain terms which cause you problems. One term is "salvation." What are you being saved from? How is this salvation applied? You need to be saved from your own fears and thoughts which prevent you from turning to God. How are you saved? Certainly not by magic or by passing your body or body parts through water, however it has been blessed. Nor is there any special plan which you must follow.

You can only be saved by turning with sincerity and earnestness to God. It is only with sincere desire to become one with God, that salvation comes. **Who you are saved from is yourself.**

Another term is the "power of the cross." The only power or magic within any of these symbols is the power which comes from your belief and faith. No person has all the answers to all questions, only God. God knows all, sees all, hears all, senses all and is in all. **God is not only our Creator, but our Sustainer and our constant Companion.** On earth, you have found it easier to pray to me or to someone else whom you have designated as a saint. When you pray to us, we must in turn take this prayer to God. There is no magic or special help which we give. We are God's creation just as you. We believe and have faith because we have tried God on many matters. **Always we have found that God hears and answers our prayer.**

Let us continue to define terms such as "prayer." Prayer is simply talking to God. **One prayer or one form of prayer is not better than another.** How do you speak to your parent, friend or child? When you have a problem and you talk it over with these people, do you start in a loud voice to plead and beg? No, you simply in a quiet voice explain your dilemma or problem. That is all you need do when you pray. Special words or a repeating of words is not necessary. Each prayer is as diverse and unique as each individual. If certain prayers, which you have learned from childhood, help you enter a mood of quietness to pray, this is good.

What I am saying to the people of earth is not to get so caught up in rituals, not to allow all the "shoulds" to keep you away from God, not to allow anything or anyone to interfere in your contacting God. No one can tell you what to do with your thoughts. There is no way for anyone to censor these thoughts but you. **The only person to keep you from contacting God is you.**

We have stated that prayer is simply talking to God, but you do not have to constantly be asking for favors. You can and should carry on a conversation with Him. Tell Him the things which puzzle you. Tell Him how you feel about certain people, such as how you feel toward your family. God knows everything anyway, so why not ask Him to intercede on your behalf? God knows all, He is waiting for you to bring everything to His attention.

My son Jesus likened God to our Heavenly Father. **God has given each of us freedom of choice in all matters,** even to give us the option of asking for His help or not, because God respects your freedom of choice. He will not interfere in any problem until you ask. He is aware of the feelings which you are building up. **Ask God to intercede, to give you a new understanding and a new way of viewing every situation.**

Another term which is sometimes confusing to people is "Heaven." You on earth consider this a place, much like your local grocery store which is in a building on a certain street. **Heaven is a state of mind.** It is not a location, but a way of viewing the events around you. Heaven is wherever you are on the earth plane or in spirit. Heaven is like a mood or mind-set. Wherever you are, you can choose to live in heavenly surroundings or in a hellish situation. Even in the spirit world there are those who live in heaven and find their life here pleasant. There are those who live in hell. It is all up to each individual.

"Oh," you ask, "why are some people constantly having such rotten luck?"

It is the attitudes in your heart and deep in your mind. People's situations are not as they appear on the surface. Only God, who sees into the hearts and minds of men, can see the truth.

You also can tell what kind of situation, heaven or hell, a person lives in. There are those who have worldly riches, but are either unhappy, addicted or unhealthy. Then there are those who are wealthy, happy and healthy. These things come from the whole belief system and the attitudes of an individual. A state of mind is made up of all a lifetime's actions and thoughts.

You have the choice to live as you like. If things are not to your liking, pray, ask God to help you see clearly, to help you set attitudes and thoughts in order to improve your life. All things are healable and all situations are amenable. **True prayer is asking God to set your life in perfect alignment with His will.** God always knows what is best for us, although it may not be what we wish to hear.

Take for instance, a parent. One does not always allow a child to act the way he wants. A parent modifies and corrects the actions which would cause a child harm. Ask God the Father to intercede, to straighten and perfect your thoughts, so that you may live in heaven here on earth, in this present time frame. This is asking for the highest and the best.

How many ways can I repeat my message to the people of Earth? What words do I use to reach your hearts, to make you feel the need to come close to God? This has been my message throughout the centuries. I have left places of healing as a testimony of my apparitions and my message. People only consider their physical bodies. They never give thought to their spiritual needs. I beg and plead with you, return to God. Allow Him to infuse your being with His Spirit.

The people of Yugoslavia have taken my message seriously and have committed themselves to prayer, meditation and worship of God. I would like for this country to do the same.

This great land was built on spiritual foundations. This America was begun because of a need to express your own spiritual worship. People of America, listen and pay attention to my words. I cry out to you to awaken and see the danger which is now upon you. Look to your hearts and see what manner of feelings and desires reside in you. What will it take for you to return to your original premise which is God? It does not matter which religion is used to seek God. It does not matter which ritual is used to find God in your heart. Go to any church or go to no church. Seek God in your heart and mind. Worship the One God of the Universe through your thoughts and with your feelings. Sing praises to Him and be grateful for life and this wonderful planet which is your home.

It is not for God's or my benefit that you should seek God. It is for your benefit alone. This should motivate your seeking of God and Truth. The dangers which are fast approaching are in the form of storms of tremendous size. Tremors will rock the earth; volcanic eruptions will become commonplace. Tidal waves will be of enormous size. The sky will stand still, or so it will appear. The stars will be moved about in the heavens. The sun will rise from a new direction. The temperature changes have already started to happen worldwide. The winds will come from nowhere and destroy much of what you have built.

This is not the end of the world. But it is the end of this era. There will be a new beginning and a new land. The people who survive will take a new stance and a new viewpoint. The world will become the Eden of old. The regeneration of land and of souls will happen with you or without you. **The only way to prepare is in your mind and heart.**

The seeking of truth and knowledge from the One God is your only hope. This hope is everywhere. All it takes to acquire this hope is to listen in meditation. By prayer seek the Love and Hope which are found in God. I do not want to alarm you unduly, but I wish to inform you of the future. I wish to inform you so that you can be prepared.

God has allowed me to appear all over the world, and in many places I will be seen. Some will hear my voice; others will see me; others will see light; others will receive a healing for their physical bodies. All this to get your attention. What else will get your attention? How many more miracles will have to be performed in order to get your attention?

Repent and seek your origin. Seek to find the gold in your hearts, instead of the gold which is of this world. My son Jesus came to give you a glimpse of this time, to prepare you with His knowledge, to lead you by stories and parables to understand the nature of the spiritual realm.

All this discussion over interpretations of the Bible is futile. All the arguments, about which religion is correct, are wasted effort. **There is only one way to find the One God and that is in your heart and through your mind.** Put aside the explanations of each Bible verse. Put aside the new word and the old word. Give up your arrogance and your prejudices. Wipe clean the thoughts of hatred and hostility. Clean up your thoughts and your inner being by asking God to help you find Him.

All He wants is the invitation to return to the communication and communion which you and He had in the beginning. The song which is in your heart was placed there on that first day you came into being. The way to find God is not lost, only forgotten or pushed aside as an old shoe. There is comfort, knowledge and a wealth of things seen and unseen in finding God in your heart and through your mind. Deep in your mind is the connection. Deep in your heart is the feeling that Truth is real and the only way to live.

Bring your sincerity and eagerness to find God, and it shall be as you desire. The outer things do not matter. Why is it important to criticize each other's ways? Why do you busy yourselves with how someone else is doing? Why worry over your brother or sister's errors? These are not your concern. Your only concern is in finding the peace and hope which are found only in God.

Go to the altar in your mind. There confess yourself to God. You will redeem yourself and make amends to God. Your connection to God will be strengthened. It is not strengthened in some building, or by another's blessing you with water, or by performing any ritual over your physical body. When your inner heart and mind are truly connected to the One God, you will find those things which are not pleasing to Him will simply fall away. Do not become upset with this bad habit or that suggestion. Do not allow someone else's opinion of how you should behave to interfere with your seeking of God. The face which you present to the world is not the face which is presented to God, for **God looks into your heart and mind and sees only truth. You cannot hide your true nature from God.** It does not matter which of your brothers or sisters have failed. It does not matter how big your donations have been. Nor does it matter what clothes you wear or what you drink or what you eat. All these things are of the outer life and of the world.

Instead look into your heart. What are you feeling: pangs of remorse, fits of anger, lecherous looks, jealousy, envy? These are the feelings which kill your spiritual nature. What of your thoughts? Are you lustful, hateful, or purposely seeking to undermine someone's best efforts? This is how to clean your house. This is what to release from yourself. This is the inner temple which needs to be cleansed in order to find God.

In the near future, there will commence storms of huge magnitude which will cause many to think the end of the world is at hand, but you will know differently! This will only be the cleansing of Mother Earth. Mother Earth is sick and crying out to God to help her heal and realign herself to be in Divine Order with the rest of the universe. These changes which will occur are universal in scope and have been taking place for many millions of years.

The universe is a constantly growing unit, as are you. In the human body many new cells are produced daily as others die. This is also true of the universe. But there are other factors which have entered to speed up this process. The use of chemicals, pesticides and other agents which have harmed and damaged the planet are speeding up this process. Some major changes will occur to ensure the viability of the planet. In other writings I have expounded on the danger of these chemicals. The soil, plant, mineral and animal worlds of this planet have been affected. So has the human family.

Not only are you contaminating the soil and life of this planet, but you have become dependant on chemicals and other drugs which interfere with the use of your mind. Man as a whole has placed his mind on automatic pilot. You have allowed others to direct the course of your lives. By becoming apathetic, you do not even see danger or recognize that you are in any danger. Wars continue to be warred in the name of God. Entire families have been torn apart by greed, anger, hatred and fear. These will also tear your world apart. All these things individually could not cause the planet to revolt. Since it is time for this era to end, the violence in which it ends is up to you collectively.

As I see it now, there will be much destruction around the planet. New land will rise up and allow the land which has been contaminated to rest for centuries. This is the only way to rid this Earth of the waste materials which are a danger to all life.

The end of this era was foreseen many years ago. My son Jesus came to earth to prepare people. To teach all to rely on God for their needs. But many have not understood his message.

There have been many wars waged because of differences in how to interpret the word of God; also to determine who has the right to enter heaven. These are all childish differences, because all came from God and all have the right to return to your true home in God. Put aside the emotions which kill the spirit. These emotions are fear, anger, envy, jealousy, hatred, prejudices and such. These emotions kill the spirit and also kill the very nature of man. The body which is filled with these emotions is sick physically, mentally and spiritually. You have the power to eliminate these emotions. You are free to choose how you will feel and when you will feel differently.

Pray as you know how, for there are as many ways to pray as there are individuals. No one prays wrong when he seeks God in his heart and mind with sincerity and eagerness. **Prayer is talking to God in your mind. Meditation is becoming quiet and still in your thoughts to contemplate the nature of God.** In quietness He will give you all His good gifts, which are of more value than anything in the world. Just know that God is more wonderful, more marvelous and so much more than you can imagine. It is in your heart and with your mind that you see Him and He sees you. Nothing is hidden from God. Therefore bring all of your concerns to Him. Pray daily and meditate often. In meditation you will increase your knowledge and your understanding of what is real and what is true.

My words are for all people, all nations and all religions. This is a global warning and not simply a national or a religious matter. The events which are already happening are happening to the whole world. Every person will be affected by the coming events. The prediction of events are of such a magnitude as to be unbelievable. Not one solitary person on earth will remain unaffected by the coming changes. The storms, earthquakes and volcanic eruptions will be of unheard of proportions.

Many of the predictions which I will give are individual, and unless all the happenings are looked at globally, you will not be able to see the pattern of events. Soon all people will know that there is something unusual happening around the earth. The skies will be telling you. The earth tremors, the animals and seas all will be screaming, "Look something unusual is happening."

It will be hard to avoid this message in a few years. The governments will have to face the truth, for the citizens will demand answers. Not all the news is reaching everyone now. There is a lot of censorship, even in your country which is so proud of its freedom of the press. The censorship is not a deliberate coverup of the truth, but it is an ignoring of important matters. The publishers do not realize what is happening yet. They think these incidences are isolated and not of value to the general public. In a few years there will be too many unusual happenings to ignore.

Mankind will be glad to have the new era to correct the errors of your civilization's past. Humanity will remember what these errors were. Future generations will learn from your mistakes as a species.

New cells will blossom in the physical body. Humanity will have communication with the spiritual world. New cells will come forth and you will be able to use more of your mind. Mankind will have powers that are not known now. There will be the ability to communicate with all worlds by your mind. Humans will also be able to communicate with the animals in this method. Truly, there will be born a new man and a new species.

Man will enter into a new period of communications with those who live in other parts of the universe. Humanity will put aside its childish fights over land. Man will take pride that as a species and a race he has grown and learned to be united with the universe. This will truly be a glorious way of life.

In future time, man will be as different from the man today as you are from the cave man. You will progress as humanity through all the tribulations. Sometimes it is through the difficult periods that the most growth takes place. Sometimes it takes the complete annihilation of the bad seed to allow the fruit to become sweet once again.

There is much happening in your world today. More will be happening which is unexplainable. This is when you will see that I tell the truth. I give you Truth as I give you knowledge.

I want to concentrate on the Spiritual Hope and the Spiritual Conversion which man must make in order to survive spiritually. This life in spirit is the serious and real life. It is important that no one digress in their spiritual growth. We must all move forward. This is only done as a whole and not as segments. The Creation of the One God is a whole, and it is this whole creation which is growing and moving forward.

God is all Love. You and every being in the universe are surrounded in his Great Love. The love of which I speak is so wonderful and so unwavering you cannot imagine how great it is. Simply go into the temple in your mind and allow yourself to feel the love which is there. Feel the gentleness which is around you. Look to the tenderness which is in you and feel the love as it grows and grows.

The tenderness and gentleness which have been attributed to me through the centuries is God expressing His loving nature through me. You can also express God's Loving nature to your part of the world.

The predictions will happen as I have stated, over the next few years. After this, there will be little doubt left in anyone's heart.

There will be a new Jerusalem as predicted in the book of *Revelation*, but first there will be some terrible events on this planet. The events will be tremendous because the populations have not taken care of this planet. It could have all been a little gentler, but due to the chemical waste and the use of all the drugs which are harming the youth, the Earth is revolting and will literally turn itself over to cleanse and to rid itself of these negative influences.

There is not enough conversion of men to bring this about in a milder form. We must remind people to return to God. To seek God in their hearts and minds. That is the only place to find God, not in rituals, religions or in certain conduct. Seek to find God inside yourself. Do not rely on priests or preachers to pave your way. God cannot be found with money. God has no use for money. It is all in vain, if that is what you think. God has no use for wild preaching on street corners. He does not need loud praying in the churches. God doesn't care about clothing. All these mandates are from men and are not from God.

God seeks only a sincere heart and the eagerness of a believing mind to be in union with you. Rely on God to answer your prayers and to give you His good gifts. Depend and trust on God to give you the Truth. Nothing is mysterious about God. Nothing is unusual about God. God made this universe, and the laws of nature, physics, aerodynamics and relativity. These are not new to Him. There are more laws of which you know not. There is more in the universe and in this world which could enhance your living, if you would but seek to learn the truth in all things.

What is not pleasing to God are war, fear, hunger, poverty, ignorance, idleness, abuses of all kinds and discussions of who is right and who is wrong about heaven, God and Jesus. God is not pleased with those who think they can tell others what He wants! God is not pleased with laziness or procrastination. These are the things which displease God. All these things come from the little minds of men. All these things come from those who are so arrogant as to believe that they can speak for God.

The message I am giving you is from me. I would not begin to try to speak for God. My message is one of concern and love. My aim is to warn the people of the world of the coming events, to give them time to find God in their hearts and to make amends, to return to their original place, to atone and to believe that all things which happen on earth will be for the good of all.

This will be hard to believe when the world is literally turning upside down. It will be hard to maintain your faith and your trust then. That is why it is so important to begin to rely on and trust God now. That is why it is necessary for all men to come to terms with their own consciousness, to accept that these events will be for the good of all, and, most of all, for the good of the planet. **My message is to instill hope, love, and care for each other and this beautiful world.**

CHAPTER

7

The Spirit of YOU

THE SPIRIT WORLD or the "other side," as some people call it, is the real world. **The real life is lived from the spirit world.** This is difficult for you on earth to realize. You have always thought of earth and your life on earth as the real world, the total sum of reality.

My son Jesus came with the message of eternal life. He demonstrated this by dying on the cross. No matter what happens to you on earth, you continue to live. Physical death is not the end of life as has been believed. Jesus' whole life was given to living the Truth of His being, which is also the truth of your being. How many times did Jesus say, "I have come to show you the way, the truth, and the life. The things I do, you can do also"?

God has given every person life eternally. When you die a physical death, it is but a passage into the real world from which you came. Life on earth is only for a few years. Life does not begin at birth and end at death. This is a fallacy in the minds of men. This mentality has been called the earth-mind consciousness.

This earth-mind consciousness is the consciousness of humanity which holds the truths believed by men over the centuries. There are many errors of truth in this consciousness. One is that you are living in reality on earth.

All life on earth is made up of molecules, atoms, protons and photons. It is made up of chemical combinations. By changing the chemical combinations, you change the appearance of the subject. By changing the chemical combinations you change reality, as it is seen on earth. Life itself is not held in a test tube. You cannot measure, weigh, or see the life-force which is in everything. That which animates everything is unseen, unheard and unfelt.

Now, perhaps, we have established that life is eternal, that life is more than you can see, hear or touch. There is a world which is unseen, unheard and unfelt by humans. See what your scientists have found through telescopes, microscopes and other machines which now can measure the waves of light and sound.

There is more to each person than is revealed in this life. There is a spirit which exists and remains in the spirit world as you incarnate. You are a spirit-self which is in the process of learning many lessons in order to gain perfection. This perfection takes much learning and much practice. Now allow me to explain that you live many lives, one at a time, and, at times, two or more at a time. Your spirit is greater than you know. There is, deep within you, a connection to the true you which is spirit.

How can you live more than one life? You can learn more than one subject at a time, is this not so? With advancement, the spirit can live more than one life at a time. The spirit-you can incarnate into different cultures, different sexes, different parts of the world. In so doing, the real you is practicing many lessons which have already been learned. Learning is the key. Learning is the whole essence of your life. Life is for learning. In working through every experience there is much learned.

The spirit-you has been called by many names: the higher self, super-consciousness, and, also, the soul by many religions. The soul is the receptacle which holds the spirit. **The spirit is the essence, the God-part of you.** It is inside the soul. The spirit is contained within the soul. The soul is your spiritual body. The physical body holds the soul, which in turn holds the spirit-you. It is through the soul that you come into the physical body, time and time again.

This is perhaps a foreign idea to many people in this part of the world, but it is Truth. There is nothing for you to do on earth to insure eternal life which all live. God gives us eternal life free, as He does air, choice and many other benefits. Eternal life is a gift from God. You do not have to do or believe anything to have this life. You already have it. You already have lived for eons, first in one body, then in another; first as one sex, then as another; first in one culture, then in another. Life is endless and eternal.

There is a part of the spirit which remains in this world or plane as it also has been called, even while you are living on earth. This spirit-you which remains here is your entire consciousness. It is that voice inside your head which tells you when you are doing "wrong." I give the word "wrong" emphasis because wrong is determined by the spirit-self.

The spirit-you which remains here keeps a record or log of all your decisions, your experiences while on earth. It is also called the book of life. God does not keep it, each spirit-self keeps its own record of all its lives, decisions, lessons and talents. Your spirit-self decides which lessons and what your lifetime goals are before you incarnate. The spirit-you judges you at the end of each lifetime and determines how you progressed, or if you have accomplished your life goals, what other lessons you learned, what other talents you perfected. It also determines what needs to be rectified.

From within the spirit-you come many talents, many strengths, many accomplishments. These could be the accomplishments which have been learned in the past. In times of need you will find these strengths, talents and abilities within. Latent abilities come forth as they are needed.

Understand that the spirit world is not an easy one to describe or to explain. There are many, many wonders which cannot be described because there is nothing like them on earth. You do not have any way of even beginning to understand. There is not a parable or anything on earth which compares to these wonders. This one idea keep with you always: there is more to life and to God's Creations than you know.

Another fallacy which is believed on earth, is that there is a heaven, a hell and a purgatory. This could possibly be a better description of how things are after death. Here in this part of God's Creation, where you come after death and before birth, all is lived mentally. It is with your thoughts, beliefs, concepts and attitudes that you create your environment. **Heaven and hell are simply mental states, both on earth and here.** What you think is what you have. If you believe you are in heaven, you will find things pleasant. If you are in fear and believe in hell, you will truly live in fear.

This world is a mental world. That means every thought is visible and brings an immediate response. Here you must watch your thoughts. There must be control of thought in order to control your life.

On earth your life is also lived by your thoughts. There is the problem of lag time on earth, which at times confuses mankind and makes him think things just happen. From your past come decisions or choices which bring on every condition. In every part of God's Creation all is ultimately lived from what you carry in your mind and heart.

In this part of God's Creation are many temples of learning. There is much activity, many new and wondrous abilities to perfect. These temples are dedicated to the teachings of God's Essence. All of us, being spirit-selves, have these abilities within us. The key is to bring them out, perfect them in theory and in practice. All you do or fail to do is a matter of choice. This is our right, given to us by God. We always have the choice in everything, here and on earth.

Allow one moment to consider this right, which is God-given: **you choose everything which is in your life.** Every moment of your life there are choices to be made. These choices, and your response to these choices, are what your life consists of. Some people make decisions by not making a choice. In deciding not to make a choice, the choice is made. You must make a choice, either directly or indirectly.

Prayer is asking God to help you. You make a choice to enlist His help. Take heart, all sincere prayer is good. The ability to give your choice to God is the best response, although in reality there are no wrong choices. By this I mean there are only your choices, and you alone must live according to your choices.

This ability to choose gives each of us complete freedom in life. No one is a puppet! See how wonderful this freedom is? Feel the freedom deep inside you; glory in this freedom.

Look at the choices you already have made. Each person on earth today has chosen to incarnate, to live on earth during this time. You have chosen your culture, your mate, your career, your personality. You chose to read this book. In the end, you will choose what to do with this information.

Now a word about this life you have chosen. Simply because you have already chosen the circumstances in which you find yourself does not in any way mean it must continue status quo.

Let us say today, you do not like where you find yourself. You are not happy with your personality, your career, your status. All these things can be changed. You realize of course, there are some conditions which cannot be changed. But everything can be improved. If you do not like your personality, improve it! If you do not like your place in society, change it, either by more education, developing your creative talents or, most important, through prayer. Do not become passive and blame destiny for the conditions of your life. There is always change, and you have the ability to improve everything and anything. Continuous change is a universal law.

The temples which are in this spirit-plane, or world, are for the purpose of helping spirit-selves to improve some area of their eternal lives. There is no tuition or requirement except that you attend. These temples are for the learning of Love, Knowledge, Wisdom, Intelligence, Strength, Creativeness and much more.

There are schools within these temples. In the Temple of Love, for instance, you find the schools of patience, tolerance, friendliness, forgiveness, sincerity, kindness, etc. I chose the example of Love because it is a very important Essence of God. All creatures are made in God's Love. This is part of the image and likeness of God in which we are all created. The Love of God is so abundant here that you actually feel it, taste it and see it. The Love of God is also abundant on earth, but mankind has ignored it for so long that he doesn't recognize it anymore.

This mentality of earth-mind consciousness has put a cloudy mist around Divine Love. It is covered in ignorance, and mankind has closed its eyes to Divine Love.

The spirit-you is the real you. **You are not your body alone.** This has been a great revelation to many women today. They have always known this in their minds, but the information has not become a part of their own awareness. They think in terms of the physical appearance as the essence of themselves, their values, and at times their worth. This is not only true of this writer but of many women in the world today. The outer appearance is all-important. Many lose their lives because they become obsessive about the outer appearance. The shape of the outer body is not you, nor does it in anyway indicate your value or worth.

There are also men today who are obsessive about their bodies. The outer appearance is not the issue. **It is the inner, spiritual-self which is the REAL YOU!**

In reality, the physical body should be maintained in good physical condition. But to place all your self-worth in the outer shape of the body is a tragic error in judgment. You are so much more than this outer physical body indicates. You have more in your spirit than you are using at any given moment. The spirit-you is filled with many talents, strengths and attributes which will make your life interesting and joyous.

The mind which you are using to read this book is also another element which is much overlooked. It contains much wisdom, knowledge and intelligence. You have only to pray to God to bring out all these attributes which are in your mind. I would love to see all people on earth mentally discipline their thoughts. In this way they could begin to live their lives in total reality, and discipline their thoughts with gentleness and love. They can and will learn to control their thoughts in time. Sooner would be better, for then they will have heaven wherever they are.

Control your attitudes and your beliefs in order to control your thoughts. Your attitudes and beliefs give your mind the pattern with which to work. Place all of your attitudes and beliefs in God. Release fear, anxiety and hatred from your mind. Live your life in the concepts which best describe God: Love, Hope, Peace, Strength, Gentleness, Faith, Abundance and Goodness.

The disciplining of your thoughts is very important to every person on earth. This is how life is lived here, and after your physical death this will be your reality. Here in this part of God's Creation your every thought brings quick results. If you think in fear, you will live in fearful conditions. Think peaceful, hopeful thoughts, and you will live life in peace and hope. There are no needs which cannot be met with your thoughts. You desire to live in a beautiful house, think it and it will be so instantly, even though in reality there is no need for a house. If you desire to harm some other being, you harm yourself instantly.

Every thought brings results. This cannot be emphasized too much! It is important to know all you can about this all-important part of yourself. The controlling of your thoughts, attitudes and beliefs is something you can practice on earth. Also, accept the fact that you live forever and ever. You do not have to do anything special to receive eternal life. It is given by God.

Prayer is also a great part of our lives here. Prayer is not only for those on earth, but also for us. We pray for you on earth. We pray for your eyes to be opened and your ears to hear these truths. In giving yourself to God in prayer, you allow His Great Being to come into your spirit-self to be in complete alignment with His Truths.

What do I mean by being in complete alignment with God's Truths? It is the best you can have, the best you can ever hope to acquire in all phases of your real life: spiritually, physically, mentally, emotionally, psychically and in many other ways. All attitudes, beliefs, and spirit are in a straight line with All that God is. The flow of God-Essence is smooth and complete. The intelligence, wisdom and judgment which you need on earth or in spirit will flow gently through you to help with all your decisions. You will have the right of way in all decisions. You will be in the flow of God-Essence. This is important to you, no matter where you are.

To be in complete alignment with God while on earth gives you an edge. You find that you are simply in the right place at the right time. Your spirit-self is flowing and swimming in God-Essence freely. Do you remember the words of Paul? "For in Him we live, move and have our being."

God is All, everything seen and everything unseen. **There is no place where we can be without being in God.**

Every person has the right to make his own choices. You pick and choose every area of your life. If you desire to be wealthy, it is your choice. A desire for health is also your choice.

This is not always evident to you on earth, for there are times a baby is born with many physical ailments. You ask, "How did this little child choose to be ill?"

Simply, dear ones, the choice was made before birth. Why does a person choose to be born with handicaps? That is not for me or you to judge. There are certain lessons and goals which are decided on before birth. Then the soul decides which conditions would best help him learn these lessons. These are spiritual lessons, and as such, it is difficult while on earth to see the value of this learning.

Why are there accidents? Because someone made a choice which brought about the accident. If it is an accident which is caused on purpose, then the perpetrator has to answer and rectify the damage which this choice caused.

Nothing is left unnoticed or to chance. Every small event, word, thought, decision or choice is noted by the spirit-self. This spirit-self is unemotional and unwavering in its diligence. It records everything to the last detail. Perhaps you will not see with your physical eyes the problems brought on by your or another's choices, but the spirit-self sees. The spirit-self brings out everything at the time of your judgment. This is not to scare you, but to warn you that all things are rectified by you. You judge yourself. That is, the spirit-self judges how the life which has just been lived helped you to learn, what decisions are to be rectified, and how they will be rectified.

Here enters another concept which is accepted in other parts of the world—that of Karma. This is another word for the concept of keeping up with all your deeds, thoughts, responses, attitudes and beliefs. This record of your deeds, in thought and in action, is kept in your book of life and is what makes up your karma.

When a murder is committed on earth, the deed, the response and the thoughts which entered into this deed are karmic. Through karma there is a rectifying of all deeds, actions, thoughts, attitudes and beliefs. But this rectifying of your past transgressions is not as easy as it seems.

Perhaps the handicapped person is rectifying some misdeed or mistake of the past. Perhaps the handicapped are simply using this method to learn a lesson, such as humility. There is much which goes into making the decision to rectify your mistakes.

There also is a time of rest. After a death, especially one which has been violent or a lifetime of violence, there is a period of rest for the soul. There are those souls who remain in a state of suspended animation for many eons. They remain so because of the life that was lived.

Hitler is one of these souls who lived such a violent life he is in a long period of complete unconsciousness. This allows the spirit to heal, to give the spirit-self time to judge itself and to regain its perspective on life. At intervals this soul is brought out of this state of suspended animation and questioned as to its perspective on life. If there is no recognition of the violence which needs to be rectified, it is returned to its unconscious state for another era or so.

In this state of suspended animation the soul does not grow or learn anything. It is inert and useless. The life-force is placed on hold, the spirit-self can only look within. This is a sad place for any soul to be. There is loss and regression of spirit. The soul finds itself in complete and total darkness.

The idea of violence is the quickest way to be in this suspended state, but be aware there are other ways to be brought to this state. A life lived in complete negativity, in which all the person sees is darkness, abusing situations, hateful thoughts, beliefs in evil and attitudes of abuse. At times, a person appears to be "good." This is because on earth you judge by outer appearances. The goodness which is seen, is that which the person allows others to see. But what of the inner person? What do you see of the spirit, of his thoughts? On earth you try to judge people, but it cannot be done in truth, because you do not hear the thoughts, or know the motives.

The judgment of men is best left to the afterlife. God does not judge us, but allows our spirit-self to sit in judgment along with the personality which is you.

Why is all of this important to know now? The importance is in the opening of your eyes and ears to reality. To allow you to become aware of the great opportunity to grow in spirit while you are yet on earth.

Soon, the Earth will have its day and move into its new position in the heavens. Many on earth will lose their physical lives and be in confusion as they return to this reality. Many will find that they are no longer living on earth and be completely baffled as to where they are.

My objective in giving this message is to give every person on earth time to learn and pray. Most often as a person crosses over into this plane, there are souls which meet him at the crossing. He is helped to adjust and acclimate to this environment, but with the millions which will be coming at one time, during the future Earth disasters, we will be hard pressed to give this individual attention. The better you are prepared mentally, the faster your adjustment. In order to reach a level of comprehension and readiness, each person is responsible for his own being.

To prepare, PRAY! Pray and meditate on God-Essence. Activate all that is in your spirit-self in this lifetime and complete your lifetime goals. It will be through prayer that you are led to the situations which will give you the experiences to reach these goals.

Yes, dear children, there is much more in the spirit world. There are many different worlds and levels to reach. But these are not important to you at this time. It is interesting, but not essential for your preparation.

Know that as you pray and meditate on GOD, you are advancing in spirit and in truth. This is the important issue. This is what you are on earth to learn. As you become aware and seek God in your heart and mind, answers to your questions will come. But the more answers you receive, the more questions you will have. The search for Truth is eternal. The seeking of God is for every lifetime.

God is more than any one person can hold in his mind with a thought. God is at the same time personal, spirit, principle and law. He is the air you breathe, as He is the life-force which animates you. God is in everything. The forces of nature are the forces of God as Law. The regeneration of nature is God as Principle. The quiet voice within you is God as Father, which is God as a Person. God as Spirit is in this world and all worlds, this life and all life.

It is easier for people to become acquainted with God as Father. In this capacity He is ever-loving, ever-gentle, ever-caring. Have faith in God, the Father for all your needs, all your goals, and your entire life. Rely on God-Principle through prayer. When you activate the principles of God through prayer, you are certainly "saved," not in the tradition of today's religions, but in spirit. You are saved from errors in judgment, thoughtlessness and ignorance.

Much is discussed on earth about sin. Sin, my children, is a spiritual mistake. You commit the biggest sin in failing to seek God, in failing to advance in this lifetime. A wasted lifetime is sad! There is nothing sadder or more wasteful. When we say nothing, we mean it is a "NO Thing." It is a life lived in complete negativity, in complete idleness of spirit—not that the person is idle on earth. Perhaps this type of person gives the illusion of great activity. He is always going somewhere, doing something, and busy. But if a person is too busy to give a little thought to his spirit-essence, he has indeed lost a whole lifetime.

See, dear children, you cannot judge what is happening in another person's mind or heart. You cannot say a person is "good," because you have no way of knowing what is in that person's mind or heart. On the outside, perhaps, he or she appears very "good," but what counts in spirit is what is in the mind, heart and soul.

This is how to live life on earth to your spiritual advantage. Prayer is of the utmost importance. Meditate on God-Truths, God-Essences and on God-Goodness. Seek to find your connection to God and the kingdom of heaven through your mind and heart. Forget the different religions and go straight to the heart of it all, to God. Look to those areas in every religion in which there is agreement.

Find time in your daily life for prayer and meditation. Place your attitudes, thoughts and deeds on a straight line with God-Truths. Appreciate the beauty in this world and strive to do your part to care for this planet which is your home. Pray for the world, for the planet and for your nation. Pray for peace to be in the hearts and minds of the leaders of this world.

There is one place all men return after the physical death. There is not a heaven for Catholics, another for Buddhists or Muslims. **We are all one family in God,** created by God, Creator of All. Put aside your thoughts of nationality and begin to think in terms of humanity. Put aside your thoughts of "my religion" and think in terms of spirituality and the Creator. Meditate on how alike all of humanity is. Pray for the whole world and every person on this planet. In this way much will be gained spiritually for all men.

We, those on earth and those in other worlds, dimensions, levels, planes, planets, are One. We are all One because we have all been created by the same Creator. We are all One because we all have the same life-force active in us. We are all One because we all live, move and have our being in God, Creator of the Universe. Pray as one body, think as one body, for in reality we are One.

8

The Importance of Prayer

(Throughout the daily messages Mary has asked us to pray. Not only for ourselves and our loved ones, but for the entire world. As we received these messages, it became clear that we did not know how and why to pray, and also didn't understand the importance of prayer.)

Prayer

IN GIVING THIS MESSAGE to the world, I have asked that all people pray, but I realize that you on earth do not always understand prayer. You think of it as pleading or begging. Prayer is many ways to communicate with the Creator God. I will give you some of the ways you pray.

Understand that **the very act of desiring a closeness with God the Father is the very best prayer,** because this is the true purpose of prayer and meditation. Start with the form of prayer you know and, as you progress in prayer, your very prayers will change. They will change as you understand more the spiritual realm. Know that **true prayer is communion with**

Father God. It is a blending of self into His Great Spirit. **It is accepting the Love which God has for us.**

Prayer is your ability to communicate directly to God the Creator. All have a need for this communication. It is as essential to your well-being as air or water. This need was placed in you by God at the time of creation. Everyone prays, even when there is no realization of the process. You are continuously communicating with The Creator. It is, however, to one's benefit to become aware of the lines of communication. **It is in your best interest to consciously open your mind and heart to God** for this spiritual nourishment, the sustenance which brings healing to your spirit, soul, mind, emotions and body. Spiritual sustenance is like no other element on earth. It is comprised entirely of the Love, Energy and Life of God. With spiritual sustenance your mind, heart and body will become whole unlike any wholeness known on earth and only like wholeness known in heaven. The heavenly wholeness is for your entire being. All aspects of your being are aided, not only that of which you are aware.

This is why prayer in one's life is the essential ingredient to survival, your survival in life eternal. The life which is lived on earth is but a small part of your entire life. **Your reality is in spirit.** It is the spirit which is made in the image and likeness of God, Creator of the Universe. Deep within the heart all are aware of this connection to spirit. Every person on earth calls on a higher power to help, in time of extreme anxiety. Often you are not even aware of this distress call, because it comes from deep within your being.

The importance of prayer is for your very survival. This implies that your survival on earth is based on your prayer. In the inner recesses of your heart, you are aware that the earthly life is one part of your entire being. The inner prayers of your heart are the communication. Physical survival is something which is instinctive in all creation, but in the day when the earth shakes and moves, you will need to know that your connection to a Higher Power is intact to be assured that this connection to God is a good connection. This will be your saving grace.

People pray in many different ways. They pray even when they are not aware of the act of praying. All people talk to themselves. The chatter within your mind and heart is prayer. This chatter is the automatic process of prayer. It brings into your life whatever it finds your mind concentrating on. What you expect, what you consider to be your worth, this is your automatic prayer. Prayer is as natural as breathing.

Listen closely to the chatter in your mind. Then you will have an idea of how you pray. When you pay attention to the lingering thoughts in your mind, you will find the reason for the circumstances of your life. To change the mind chatter is to change your life.

To simply say "think positive" is not enough, because there is an automatic process to prayer. The inner thoughts which you hide from others are brought forth automatically. That is how a person who seemingly "thinks positive" can have so many problems. He perhaps is not thinking the same in his inner-self. The words spoken in the outer must agree with that which you believe in the inner heart and mind. **Your automatic prayer will always produce the very conditions it finds in your inner mind and heart.**

Begin now to make an assessment of your life and find the reason for its situations and conditions. Perhaps they are due to the automatic process of your inner chatter. A major step in eliminating the causes of unhappiness, anger and war is in the self-assessment of each life.

To make a concerted effort to seriously take a look at that which you hold dear is a very big step in cleansing yourself. This is not only a big step but an all-important step. Many people pray by rote. They never take a good look at those hard feelings they hold to others. Jesus said, "Why look at the mote in your brother's eye and ignore the log in your own eye?"

Ferret out all the hurts, the causes of snide remarks towards your neighbor. Critique your inner feelings towards your world. Cleanse from your heart and mind any feeling of envy, jealousy, anger, unforgivingness, prejudice and such hard emotions. These emotions deplete your energy and your life. I speak of the inner life. Do not allow these kind of emotions to linger in you. Begin now to acknowledge that all people are the product of the ONE God. We are all in life together.

God is whole and is All. He is unchanging, in that there cannot be any improvement in God, but there is always change in God's creations. Even though there is change, realize and understand that God does not change in this respect: **His approach to us is to allow us complete freedom of choice.**

Keep in mind that you can have anything in your life you desire. Enter your prayers into the positive side. Ask for healing, plenty, love and serenity in relationships.

You can also enter your prayers into the negative side by worrying, by visualizing the negative or down side of any situation. If you worry instead of pray, then be aware that worry becomes your prayer. By worrying you are automatically praying for the very thing you are worrying over. When you "what if" any situation, you are asking for the very conditions you do not want. This is what many people do and usually the scenario is all in negative overtones. Or "what if," and then they go on to paint a dreary picture in their minds. Remember that this also is prayer. In this way, you actually pray for what you do not want in your life.

Prayer is talking to God in your very own way. Perhaps it is through images, music, word, or paintings. You pray as you think of your own life, as you think of your world and those who inhabit it. Most people pray using all these methods. While listening to music, they envision scenes or allow their minds to build images of happiness. Or, while listening to music, they become sad and see dark and dreary images. Remember that these feelings are prayers. When music moves you with feelings of joy, peace or love, this becomes your request. Then music itself becomes your prayer.

As you observe a painting, or create a painting, or any object of art, you pray. Sculptures, paintings or any work of art causes good or bad impressions. Realize these very impressions become your prayers. As with all works of art or all images which lie in your mind, the very image and the feelings the image brings forth become your request.

You may ask then, why is it that when someone prays for something bad to happen to another, it does not? Because this kind of prayer is not honored. Your thoughts of harm to another cause you more harm than they will anyone else. **What you think of others becomes your prayer for yourself first.** How you view your family and friends is how you are praying for them.

Take care that, as you think of your life, you are grateful for what you have. Gratitude is prayer. When you enter a mental or emotional state of gratitude, you are asking of God. As the Provider, **God replenishes your life with what you are.** When you think of a person and are grateful for the friendship, know that this is a prayer for the friend and for the friendship. When you are happy and grateful for some item or condition in your life, this is prayer. When you observe abundance of material wealth in another, be grateful and realize that what God has given this one, He can also do for you. There are no shortages in God's abundance. **Become grateful in mind and heart for all demonstrations of good. This is true prayer.**

All thoughts, feelings and words are prayer, because through these you are constantly in touch with the Universal Creator. **To have power in your prayer requires thought, concentration, and certainty.** There is power in your thoughts which comes from your mind and heart. Many call it electrical energy, mind power or vibrational power. It does not matter what this power is called, because through this power you are communicating with God, the Father.

The random thoughts, which are filled with anger, harm you. The old hurts, the inner seething, those inner feelings of depression are prayers. These kinds of prayers cause you much harm. That is why Jesus said, "Let your word be yea, yea or nay, nay."

This includes your thoughts. The inner grumbling and complaints are prayers which bring these very conditions to your life.

The mind can be thought of as an arm. The heart can be considered the other arm. So to embrace spiritually, you use the mind and heart as arms. The power to embrace spiritually is the power of prayer. Through prayer you can embrace the whole world. It is in this innermost part of you that you truly pray.

The most important item in prayer is truth. Truth is that which is true of God. To remind yourself of who you are, a creation of The One God of the Universe, is true prayer. Statements of Truth are the highest form of prayer. When you can align yourself to God in this manner: **I am a creation of the One God of the Universe, He who created everything,** you have connected to the Powerful Mind of God. In connecting to the Mind of God, all answers to all questions are found. Remind yourself daily of your true value and your true place in God's Creation.

Now let me say this about truth. Oftentimes people or religions decide they are the only ones who have the real definition of truth. But truth is true no matter what the circumstances, conditions or who is involved with the truth. Truth stands alone. Truth and God are One. So prove the truths which are given to you. If it is true of God, it is truth. What is true of the Creator is Truth. We know that God is love, so all things which are loving are truth. God is the only one who can give life. In this way you can prove truths.

God does not need to change, you do! **God does not need prayers, you do!** God is the Source of all Good. Another way of saying this is that God and Good are synonymous. You cannot have good, truth or love without having God present. It is you and this world who are in need of the elements of God. God already is All. God the Father is complete and whole. When I say whole, I am saying that in God there are no minuses. There are no needs and certainly there are never any depletions. As a Whole Being, God has everything, is everything and can supply everything. As a Whole Being, God is.

Can you appreciate the message in this sentence? *God is.* Can you see that **prayer then is for your benefit and for the benefit of every creature on earth?** Prayer is to bring your mind and heart into the Oneness of God.

People on earth, and we who are in the spirit world, have a need for meditation and prayer. It is our life-line. It is our sustenance. When you find fear, anger and these kinds of destructive emotions in your heart or as thoughts in your mind, then know that the life-line to God's Essence has been cut from your side. There is a kink or a block of some kind in you. Perhaps there is a concentration on need, depletion, fear or hatred in your mind.

God does not have these kind of thoughts. There is no fear in God. He does not recognize fear. **God simply turns fear into courage, depletion into plenty, hatred and anger into love and forgiveness.** These kind of strong emotions cannot remain the same in the presence of God. This is what happens when you bring your fearful heart to God. He is the One who gives you courage. In fearful circumstances, when you connect to God, you will find courage. In the presence of hatred, when you connect to God, you find love. When things are dark and dismal, you find light and hope. This is prayer. Bring to God what is in your mind and heart. He will change the conditions to good. The asking is for your mind to accept the changes which will come. If a situation causes you to fear, simply acknowledge the fear and give it to God to replace with courage.

Here are some steps to take to easily change your angers and hard emotions:

1. Acknowledge what is in your heart and/or mind.
2. Release all that is in your heart and mind completely to God.
3. Expect a better condition or circumstance, because God only gives improvements.
4. Give sincere gratitude.

God only changes us for our good. God cannot give us anything but good. God is good and this is all God is! Can you understand that God can only give what HE is or has Himself? It is an impossibility for God to be anything but good, because GOOD is the nature of God. Good is all that is in the Father's storehouse.

The flood of good which God sends is for our spiritual good. The first good you receive is for your true life which is your spiritual life. After you have been spiritually blessed, the earthly, physical life is aided. God's good enhances us spiritually, mentally, emotionally and physically.

Good, as God gives, is for our total being. God is as interested in your physical life as He is in your spiritual life. Many times I speak of the spiritual life and the physical life as separate lives. This is for your understanding, to give you notice of the many levels of your being. In truth you live the spiritual life along with the physical life. It is lived at the same time. Your entire being is interconnected, only your spiritual life is eternal and is not over with when the physical existence ceases. It is at the end of each lifetime on earth that we make our assessments and judgments. But this has been addressed. Pray therefore for your entire being.

When you have emotional problems, they are not separate, they are your problems. When you have a mental concern, it is your concern. You are a mental being as well as an emotional, spiritual and physical being.

There are also many other aspects of your entire being. You are an ethereal being, an astral being, a psychic being and much, much more. All these aspects are you. All are interconnected and all are important aspects of your total being.

God does not punish anyone. He does not have to! We are our own worst critics. In their hearts, people are more critical of themselves than they are of others. God sees this and allows each to judge himself. Humans expect perfection in themselves and in others. By expecting perfection, we are not tolerant of the mistakes others make. People have such a difficult time with imperfections. They will close their eyes to the imperfections in themselves, and concentrate on the imperfections in others. Yet when everyone comes to judgment day, you cannot deny the imperfections in your being.

How does anyone attain any degree of perfection? Through much, much prayer and meditation. Also by being loyal, tolerant, compassionate and loving with yourself and with others.

Admiration as Prayer

Admiration is another way we pray. Through the act of admiration, you are in a state of prayer. Now I speak of true admiration and not envy. When you look at nature, at the animals, and admire the life in them, then you are praying. True admiration is an act of appreciation and virtue. All things on earth or in space are God's Creation and to be admired. As you admire the talent in another, you are admiring the innate talent in all of us, which is God.

Prayer is not only requesting, but many other elements. Something happens when you enter into the state of admiration. It happens inside you and in what you admire. You not only appreciate, but you show love—not romantic love, but an innocent and virtuous love of that which you admire. In admiring nature you are showing God the love which you see in nature. In admiring a person you are appreciating the creation which is God-made. In admiring a talent, such as art or music, you are appreciating the inner ability which is God-given. So admiration then is prayer.

Admiration aids growth. When you admire someone's talent, you pray for it to grow. When you admire another person, the love and affinity is felt and grows. Admiration is like a fertilizer which you spread upon your life. It is truly prayer.

Now allow me to caution against envy. Envy is one of those strong emotions which depletes and causes a blockage in your being. Envy causes not only *your* good to be depleted, but the energy of those whom you envy. Envy makes the statement "I do not believe in my own abilities."

Envy suggests to your mind that you are lacking in some way. In truth no one is lacking, because in truth we are all spiritual beings, creations of the One Great God of the Universe who gives wholeness to all, attainable and possible in every being, in every world, and in every level of existence.

Joy as Prayer

Another form of prayer is joy, pure joy. Happiness and joy are ways people pray without knowing that they pray. When you are happy, you are grateful. Where there is joy and humor in life, sadness is eliminated. I speak of humor which is not directed to anyone's failings or at the expense of another person. Humor brings an element of lightness into every situation and circumstance. To look at life with humor, you are showing your confidence in God's care. It is easy to be lighthearted and carefree when you do not have worries, and in reality you do not have worries when you recognize your connection to God and to His Love. In maintaining joy and happiness within you, you are creating according to God's plan.

God's plan for each of us is GOOD. We are the ones who see life as difficult. We are the ones who take a dim view of life. People hold on to their problems as a cherished prize. Loosen your hold on problems, allow joy and humor to enter into your life. As you open your mind to humor, joy, happiness, you are aligning with God.

Through the ages people have tried to bring joy into their lives through outer influences: drink, drugs and all manner of concoctions. These outer things do not give joy. True joy is an inner quality attained from being AT ONE with God. When you have truly connected to God, you find an inner joy which is uplifting and healing.

Strive to be in alignment with God. Make this your goal. To be AT ONE with God is to be in complete alignment with Him. To be aligned means to be in a straight line with God, to be aligned with His Power and Love. There will be no angles blocking you from God, through prayer. **Prayer is placing yourself in right alignment to receive the flow of all of God's Essence.**

God's Essence is All Good; all the Good you can think of and then more. What do you consider good? I speak of **love**— pure unconditional love; **courage,** not a facade, but true courage to be able to withstand anything, to see anything, to handle anything which comes into your life, to be completely fearless, even if the earth is moved from one place to another; **hope,** not the hope of movies or stories, but true hope which knows that God is your help in all situations; **strength,** inner strength, which comes from God and does not fall by the wayside when things get tough, the ability to keep on keeping on, to arise in the morning and put one foot in front of the other; **peace,** the

inner peace which is sincere and deeply felt, not just the ability
to remain calm, but to know deep within you that All is Well
because God is with you; **energy,** not like any energy which you
receive from a pill or substance, but the inner energy to live life
fully, to overcome barriers and barricades set up by your own
mind.

There are still more elements of God: happiness, wisdom,
intelligence, enthusiasm, joy, guidance, protection and all you
could ever need. To be in alignment with God then allows the
flow of these energies or elements into your inner being.

This does not in any way denote that life will be without
problems. It simply means that **within you is all you need to
confront every situation or circumstance.** To be in alignment
with God is to be right with God, to be open to the flow of God
into your life. And this is the purpose of prayer.

Now we have only spoken of prayer and the benefits of
prayer in your life, but no man is an island. We are all interconnected. What you do to improve yourself, improves all
people. We are truly one genuine and complete Whole. When
I say we, I speak of people on earth and in every plane, level or
place in God's Creations. There are many levels of existence in
God's Creation. There is still much more to God's Creation. God
did not die. He continues to create and to live. God is ever-pres-
ent and ever-creating, and all of these creations in the Universal
Cosmos of God, are a part of the Whole. **There are worlds
within worlds, heavens within heavens and universes within
universes.** There is so much more, so many places in God's
Creations.

God is alive, dear children. He did not simply create this
world and then go off to some distant place to rest. God is active
and always creative. All of these creations are one whole unit.
In this wholeness, we are all one in God. Our link is through
God. **Our whole, eternal life is lived in God.** So know that to
pray for yourself is not self-serving, but is all incorporating to
the whole.

As you cleanse from your mind all fear and anger, it is cleansed from the collective mind of humanity. As you pray for peace to enter your mind, it is entering the collective mind also. Keep the thought that all prayer increases the thought of good in the collective mind of earth.

Pray also for others, not only for those who are your loved ones, but for all people, because all people are the creation of God. Now perhaps you understand that we are truly all interconnected and interdependent. As you advance through prayer, the whole unit is advanced. As you prepare for all events in your future, all people are prepared. This happens whether they are aware of it or not.

Pray for your preparation and for the preparation of all people. Pray for this world especially. Pray for the planet as a being. The planet will undergo many tremendous and violent changes. It will be a strain on her; it will change not only that which is on earth, but the very core of the planet itself. Pray for this beautiful planet in this great Cosmos. This is my request to each of you who read this book or who hear of these messages: **pray for yourself, for your people, and for this planet.**

Pray in your own way. If you are accustomed to using a prayer book, do so. But allow one word of caution: make sure you are sincerely feeling the meaning of the words you speak. Words spoken in rote are not prayer and will not be of any benefit. Your prayers must be heartfelt, and your total concentration must be on your prayers.

Pray in whatever position you are accustomed to. Use candles, incense or any other item which helps you become quiet and serene within yourself. Then pray in your own way. You may pray also by simply opening your mind and heart to God with words or with feelings.

Meditations

I wish to address the subject of meditation alone and separate from prayer, but realize that meditation is also a form of prayer. Through the blanking of your mind and allowing God-Mind to enter into your thoughts, you are truly praying.

Consider that **meditation is the ability to become quiet, not only in your thoughts, but in your very soul.** In meditation you allow God to fill your entire being with His Wholeness.

Meditation also has many different components. It is a complete quieting of mind and soul. It is the contemplation of a word or Essence of God. It is, at times, a chant or the quieting of your mind and inner stirring of your heart through sound, or the quieting of your inner-self through visions. The visions can be man-made or God-Made. By this I mean you can peer deeply into a painting or into the beauty of a rose. The vision could also be a vision of your mind, one which is only in your mind. It could also be a concentration on lights generated by outside forces, or lights which are only seen in the mind.

Meditation is the complete quieting of your entire inner-self. In this quietness you allow your soul to be placed in a state of idleness of mind and body. This state of meditation takes much practice. It takes time and fortitude, for the mind is tricky and will simply overwhelm you with thoughts, images and visions. You will not only see visions, you will hear sounds and feel many new and different sensations. Allow me to reassure you that this will not lead to your mind being possessed by any evil being, for remember there is no principle or power greater than God. And through the act of meditation, you invite His Great Spirit to become One with your entire life. Now it is not that God does not access your life, it is simply that God allows each freedom of choice. This freedom of choice includes the freedom to communicate with Him.

Another form of prayer is a releasing of all thoughts, feelings, sounds and concerns. This is a difficult task, but one which will help you tremendously to be in communion with God in ways not available to you through other means. Allow me to give you some instruction in this process.

The first step is to choose a special time which can be honored, when you can go apart from those in your household, a time of deep communion with God. Choose the time, and then keep this appointment with God. This can be daily, biweekly or weekly, as you choose. The important issue is to keep a set time. This process of maintaining your appointment is one which will help your mind to enter the meditation easier, for at the appointed time, your mind will become accustomed to entering the meditation. Then it is imperative to be faithful to your appointment.

The length of meditation will vary according to your needs and desires. It does not have to be a long meditation at first. Soon you will find that as the appointed time nears, your mind has already begun the preparations for meditation. The mind itself will aid you in becoming faithful to this form of prayer.

The next important issue is to **choose a place which is away from distractions,** a place which is quiet and undisturbed. Instruct your loved ones of your intention to meditate and tell them not to disturb you. The place should be comfortable, well ventilated, and the condition of the room should be warm, with no drafts of cold air.

You may either sit in a comfortable chair or the floor. The body is to be placed in a comfortable position, one which you can maintain for awhile. Remove all distractions from your environment and keep the noise level to a minimum. Most people would find that when they lie down to meditate, they quickly fall into a deep state of sleep. For this reason I recommend the sitting position. Many people find kneeling or leaning on an altar rail comfortable.

Now we have the meditation set for a definite time, the room has been prepared and the loved ones have been instructed. We will proceed, for this is an important form of prayer. All preparation has been completed.

At the designated time, enter your special meditating place. Mentally select a special scenario which denotes peace and tranquility. The scene can be by the seashore, or in a meadow or mountainside, any place you have been that gives you the feeling of serenity. This part simply aids your mind to enter into a meditative state.

Become aware of your body, by giving praise and thanksgiving to God for each part which comes to mind. Then concentrate on your breathing while you release tension and relax.

In the beginning you will find that many thoughts will enter your mind. Do not fight these thoughts, because to resist the thought is to give it power. Simply allow the thought to run its course. If at first the thoughts run wild, do not become too concerned and give up. Simply be aware that in the beginning, it will be as if your mind has gone amuck. You will find images of people whom you had forgotten entering your mind. Forgive them and yourself of any wrong doing. Two words will suffice: **forgiveness** and **love**. Whatever thought enters your mind, think forgiveness and love. Perhaps you find that this is how you spend much of your meditation time. Take as long as necessary to work through this procedure, for to forgive and send love to people is a way to pray. If it is an inanimate object or a scene which comes to mind, forgiveness and love also. As you forgive and love everything and everybody in your life, you are cleansing your inner-self of much rubbish.

One day you will enter your meditation and find your mind is quieting, but your sensing mechanism is overloaded with feelings. You may feel your entire being is one great sensation. The same procedure will work—forgiveness and love—to all feelings.

Or perhaps your mind is overcome with sounds. Do the same, forgiveness and love to all sounds. Every sense will empty its storehouse of all rubbish. These are the thoughts and feelings which are interfering with your direct communion with God, not that God is limited by these, but the human, earthly person is limited by these thoughts and feelings.

You may find that it helps to have soft, soothing music playing quietly in the background, or if this is too much of a distraction, forego the music. Each person will find his needs are different for meditation. Some will be enhanced through music, others will find candles help, others will have a need to enter a church or kneel at an altar. Whatever your inner-self needs in order to meditate, then do not analyze the outer trappings. Simply go to the heart of the matter, which is the prayer and meditation.

In pure and true meditation there is a nothingness of all sensations. When you can accomplish this feat, you will find that you are tapping into the Great Essence of God. You will find that answers to problems will come to mind at the appropriate times. And this is what you are aiming for: to find your answers, your guidance from God.

Every person needs to make time to practice this method of communion with God, because difficult events are still in the future. The harsh storms and the trembling and shaking of earth are yet a little while off. It is in preparation for the coming events that I give this message, that each person may prepare. Each person will have the time to put prayer and meditation into practice. This communication with God will see you through the coming difficult events. **Prayer and meditation are for the improvement of your whole, entire spiritual-self.**

The practice of prayer and meditation will be a great help to you in the coming days. Through your mind and in your heart, God will guide you. Not all people will continue life on earth. There will be many who will complete their earthly existence, but you know that you continue to live. You will simply be returning to your home. If it is your choice and God's will for you to continue to live on earth through these trying

times, then this will be your life-line. Be aware that this is your
life-line, whether on earth or in the spirit world.

One of the most important reasons I have come to request
your prayers and meditations is that as you pray, you erase
from the collective consciousness of man all hard emotion and
fear so that in entering a new era, the collective consciousness
of man will be as pure as possible. God can and will erase much
of the fear, anger and hard emotions, but through your prayers
and meditations you will be preparing not only yourselves but
the consciousness of mankind. The collective consciousness of
man is in need of your prayers. This consciousness is made up
of all the lingering thoughts, beliefs and attitudes of man
throughout the ages.

The future generations will find that their belief systems
will not be as overloaded with hard, frightening thoughts. Most
of the anger, prejudice and warring will be eliminated. Your
children and your children's children will have a better world,
a cleaner consciousness.

This you can do in two ways, through praying and erasing
these same emotions from your inner-self, and by praying for
your world. As you release and cleanse from your mind, it is
being done unto the race consciousness. And if you specifically
pray for the world, it will aid the process. To specifically pray
for the collective consciousness of man will bring future generations many benefits.

Meditate often with the word PEACE, for through peaceful
thoughts and with a peaceful nature you will be guided
through all events in your life.

Meditate often with the thought of LOVE, and begin to feel
the great love which is in this world, the love which was used
to create this beautiful world. Allow the Love of God to enter
your being, to enter your life and to enter your relationships.
Simply begin a meditation with this thought: God, I open my
mind and heart to your wonderful Love. Know that as you open

your mind and heart, it is also entering into the collective consciousness of mankind for all future generations.

Faith

Faith is very important in your life. Faith is the substance of answered prayers. Without faith your prayers would only be a repeating of words. Faith in what you cannot see, hear or touch is very difficult, I understand, but then, spirit is unseen. To work with the very Spirit of God is to work with the unseen, unheard essence.

Faith is the substance, the key. Substance is an indication that something can be measured, that it has mass. But the substance of which I speak is not measurable. It is not seen, but it can be sensed. You simply know in your heart that you believe. This creates a feeling of substance. And truly **your faith is what gives your prayers their substance.** It is the feeling, the belief, the attitude which creates the substance of your faith. Faith can be considered the building blocks which God uses to answer your prayers. Faith keeps you connected to God-Mind from which all answers flow.

Many times while Jesus was on earth he said, "Your faith has made you whole."

He would ask, "Do you believe I can do this?"

Because without the faith of the person who is in need, nothing can be done. So your prayers are answered according to your faith. Do you pray believing? Or do you pray with doubt in your heart?

Faith is a mental attitude. It's the attitude which insures that no matter what I cannot see, or what I cannot hear, I believe. I believe without doubt that my prayers are now being answered, not in some far off future time, but now, this moment in time. God is All Powerful, this I believe. God can heal me and the world, this I believe.

What do you truly believe? What is the attitude of your belief? What do you expect to happen when you pray? Do you pray with fear in your heart? Do you have doubts? Do you allow anger to enter your heart while you pray? This will work against your receiving the answer you desire. Put all doubt out of your heart by praying to overcome your fears. Pray to have your faith made strong. Ask God to help you understand His Goodness.

Does this sound phoney? It is not! **God loves each person on earth with a Love which is Divine and uncompromising.** God will help increase your faith, to overcome fear. His help is available to you to clear away all doubt. When you understand the Great Love of God, then all fear will dissipate. When you can comprehend the Goodness of God, you will not doubt. There will be no need for you to doubt or feel fear.

Your faith is expressed in many ways. By the confidence you have in God and Spirit. By the confidence you have in yourself. Faith is akin to trust. Do you trust God to give you only good? Do you trust God to provide for you? Prayers without faith are a vain repetition of words. The mere repetition of words will not bring answers into your life, or help.

Faith comes from the heart. It is a feeling of trust, confidence, an attitude of expectancy. This is why Jesus asked beforehand, "Do you believe I can do this?"

He was asking, "Do you trust me? Do you have confidence in me? Can you believe enough to expect this miracle will happen?"

The blind were able to see, the lame could walk, and the dead were called forth into physical life. All this because of faith in Jesus' word. It was confidence and trust in God which enabled Jesus to be successful. **Their** faith made them whole, not Jesus' faith alone, but their faith along with Jesus' faith opened the gates of heaven to the miracle.

Now Jesus said, "The things I do, you can also."

Why is it that no one has been able to accomplish these feats? Because it takes faith, trust and confidence in God. It takes the ability to see the innate Goodness which is God's nature. It requires the trust to go out on a limb, so to speak—to step out and call on your faith and the faith in the hearts of those for whom you pray.

People still look for Jesus to return to bring these same kinds of healing into the world. But these same healings are available to all, through faith, through prayers backed with faith.

Jesus had confidence and trusted God entirely, but it took the faith of the person seeking the healing to complete the circle which brought the healing. It required the ability to trust completely, to remain steadfast to this belief, and then confidence in God to bring the healing. It was easy for Jesus to trust God. He could trust completely and totally in God because Jesus knew the Love and Goodness of God. He told of this over and over.

Faith is an energy in the heart which enables the answers to prayer to enter our lives. It does not take much energy of faith to bring results. And faith as an energy can be increased. **You increase your faith through use,** through the ability to begin to understand the Goodness of God.

When you can put the image of an angry and capricious God out of the heart, you will gain in faith. When you can begin to see the Goodness of God, you will increase your faith. When you begin to get a glimpse of the Great Love God has for this world, you will trust. You will have the faith to move mountains.

So pray and meditate for this world with faith. **Trust God to give only good.** No matter what happens on earth, how the Earth moves or shakes, maintain your faith in the Goodness of God. Know that all events, no matter how frightening, are for the good of this world, that we are one with God and we are one in God.

CHAPTER

9

The Aftertime

"I like to think of the coming new era as the aftertime, for truly it will be the aftertime when all will live in peace."

Mary, Mother of Jesus

IT IS TIME for an evolutionary period to come to earth. The coming era in mankind's life is a time of evolution. This will be a period of great growth in the species of man and many species of animal. Some animals which are on earth now will not survive the coming changes. They will go the way of the dinosaur and mammoth. Man will change drastically. He will evolve into a new species.

This evolutionary process will come about because of the need to adjust. The atmosphere will change in components. The solar system will be different. A new sun will be added. This will be a binary solar system. The two suns will activate cells which will draw nourishment from the sun's rays. The need to ingest foods will be aided by the nourishment derived from the sunrays.

Man will evolve into a more mental being. He will be able to hear sounds which are not presently heard. He will see through particles of light which are hidden to him now. With his mind, man will hear and speak. He will have better use of his psychic abilities. That which you call intuition will be strongly activated in all of mankind. There will be a need for honesty because of the ability to hear mentally. Today man hides his feelings and thoughts. In the aftertime, man will not be able to hide his feelings or random thoughts. Motives will be known. All dealings will be understood. All thoughts will be heard.

Can you see how wonderful this new way of life will be? Mankind will become peaceful out of necessity. How could you approach another in anger or with malice in your heart? All feelings, all thoughts will be sensed and heard by everyone. People will learn to live in peace. There will not be any ambushes or surprises. When there is no need to hide, hiding will be eliminated. Hurt feelings will be dealt with immediately because the very openness of each situation will demand it. People will not be fooled into making compromises which are not in their best interest.

Love will be the answer to all problems, because anger and fear in problems will be seen for what they are. People will speak from the standpoint of love and compassion. Forgiveness will be the accepted mode of conduct. When a person is loving and feels remorse, others will react in love and forgiveness. Like begets like. Love and forgiveness will beget more love and more forgiveness.

Due to his increased mental abilities, man will be able to heal himself.

Man will not be able to fool even himself. There will be an openness about your feelings and thoughts. There will be no need to blame others for your shortcomings. When you can read another's mind, you will not abuse him as readily. Children will come into a newly evolved family with more mental abilities. They will teach their parents to act and react in love and from a standpoint of peace.

My children, the Light of God will shine into every man and into every situation. Where there is light, there cannot be darkness. God's Light will shine into the hearts and minds of all men. Each person will know that in order to progress, he is dependent on others; therefore, every person is important. Every person will have his place in society. All people will be needed in order to advance and to live comfortably.

The cooperative spirit in every person will come about through his survival instincts. You realize that each person has strong survival instincts. In order for the species to survive, man will learn to live in harmony and in peace. There will not be the large population there is today. The number of humans on earth in the beginning of the new era will be diminished. People are not completely ignorant. Every species has evolved because of the necessity to adjust, in order to survive.

Man will have an improved view of nature. The planet will be loved and cared for; man will not abuse the Earth. He will learn new ways to live on earth, to care for the planet and to allow for the regeneration of life on earth.

There will be pockets of technology left on earth. Those who survive in these pockets of technology will have a new attitude towards life. What is and is not important to man will be contemplated. The technology which remains will be used to improve life on earth. War and fighting will be deemed barbaric and archaic. Man will not enjoy destruction of any kind because of the amount and proportion of destruction sustained during the changes. There will be a new appreciation of life, of individual people, of the old and of the young. Each will have value to society for different reasons. The old for their know-how, the young for their strength. All will cooperate in making life on earth peaceful and heavenly.

As man evolves into a new species, so will music, art forms and beliefs. The good of today's era will be remembered in song and in art. The tales of this era will be told and retold. These times will become legends. How you live now will be buried underneath the earth. In future days, the items you treasure today will become relics. When uncovered, the new species of man will wonder how so many people could live on earth at one time.

New ways of utilizing the two suns will spark new advances in technology. There will be new modes of travel, new ways to heat your homes. The needs of mankind will change. The changes which are coming will be great. New elements will be discovered. New methods of communicating with other planets will be set into motion.

After the Earth has changed its position in space and the new sun has taken its place, then will be the time of peace which has been prophesied. In this new era, there will be communication between the spirit world and earth. People will be able to communicate with those who are living in the spirit world. In this way much insight will be given. The people on earth will have more understanding of how the universe works and of their mission on earth.

Can you imagine communicating with your loved ones who are no longer on earth, who have "died"? Think of the knowledge which will be available. Fear of death will become passé. There will be a way to talk to those who can give people knowledge of past cultures, of past abilities. Think how helpful this will be!

A person desires to cook some delicacy for which a former member of the family was famous. The past family member can be reached and help is yours. Or more importantly, say you desire to know something of the history of your family. See how easy this will be.

Also your questions about life, spirit, soul and reality can be answered instantly. There will be no need for any unanswered questions.

Jesus will be able to teach as he did while on earth. Buddha can give the explanation of his teachings.

Because of this ability to communicate with other levels of existence there will be much help in every form for mankind. The children will have lessons from people who made the discoveries of what is being taught, or, as in science, the Einsteins will be the teachers. See how wonderful the new era will be.

People will want to live in peace and cooperate with nature and each other. Mankind will desire peace and serenity. All of mankind will work for peace. When there is an eruption of temper, it will be settled quickly and with all kinds of help, spiritual and otherwise. The new species of man will be programmed deep within to live in harmony with himself and with the planet.

With each generation there will be small changes in appearance. The future man will be taller and stronger than this species. As the body changes, due to new functions of the skin, the clothing humans wear will change drastically. People will see each other's auras and hear each other's thoughts. Through the ability to see an aura you will know instantly how a person is feeling.

I like to think of the coming new era as the aftertime, for truly it will be the aftertime when all will live in peace.

The planet itself will have a new face. There will be new lands which will appear from beneath the oceans. These lands, which have laid fallow for millions of years, will rise and be fruitful once again.

Because of the changes in atmosphere, there will be new plant life on earth. The plants and foliage of today will change into new plants and new species of plants. Some hybrids will become annuals. Some foliage will disappear completely. Trees will have new forms and shapes. Trees will develop from some of the plants which are now simply bushes. All these changes in foliage will occur due to the changing gases and atmospheric conditions.

The existing plant life of earth will adapt and change. New plants will appear and some old plants will change so drastically that they will seem as new plants. Flowers will become edible. Plants will not only look beautiful but also nourish in different methods than today. Poisonous plants will have a different hue to them; this will alert man to their potential danger.

All this will take time, for as the new lands emerge from the ocean floor there will be a need for it to dry and to air out. The land will be rich in minerals and form much beauty. New rivers will form and the waters of earth will run in different directions. New oceans will form, some will have new names and there will be a remembrance of old oceans in name.

In the early days of the aftertime there will be much moisture in the air. With ash and dust in the atmosphere there will be many days with no sun. The growing seasons will be turned around and plants will grow slowly at first. Then, as the moisture gives way to the regulation of climate, there will commence a new growing season.

In the first days, as the lands settle and rearrange themselves, there will be turmoil and distress among men. Those who are relying on God, will be led to safe places. Through your mind and heart, or another way to say this, through your thoughts and feelings, will come those ideas which will direct you correctly.

There will be safe places on earth. There will be pockets of technology left intact. In these safe areas will be food, clean water and shelter. The climate in these safe areas will remain stable and in good order. The climate in the new lands will be changeable and unsettled. But these new lands will not be inhabited for some time. The climate, plants, and animals will be the order in which life will return to these new lands.

In the beginning the climate will be unsettled, then there will be a calming into seasonal patterns. Plants will spring up. Rivers and lakes will settle into their beds. As the plants begin to grow, small birds and animals will enter into the new lands. As the wind scatters seeds and life through the new land, forests will commence to grow. Seasons will be in place and the growing patterns will emerge. These lands will be untouched by man; they will be virginal and grow according to new growth patterns which will be activated by nature. Birds will migrate once again and new species of birds will enter life on this planet. Small animals will begin to move into the forest. As there will not yet be any large predators, their numbers will flourish.

As the food chain begins to expand and grow, so will mankind, but through this time of growth, there will be a remembrance of the old days. Songs will tell the young of the past era, of ancestors who lived in much fear and with hatred. The songs will explain how anger and hatred can kill the soul. Legends will spring up as time passes.

New people will populate Earth. These people will be a new species of man, as I have told you. The new species will be more aware of the spirit and soul. He will be closer to the Divine, for he will retain a remembrance. All men will be considered brothers. Love and goodwill are the elements which will be in vogue. Peace will be the rule of the day—peace with man, with nature and with God.

This will be the era of "one thousand years peace" which has been foretold. Man will have declined in numbers and will abhor anything which will take away from the population. As there will be direct communication with the spirit world, much knowledge will be gained. The new species of man will be more intelligent, knowledgeable, and understanding. He will teach patience, kindness, and forgiveness to the young. Since the young will be raised in love and peace, this is what they will practice in their lives.

Man will not only communicate with spirit but with the animal kingdom. The animals hold much knowledge and will teach man much in the ways of nature. Animals will teach man which plants and herbs they use for medicines and for food. Man will teach the animals about spirit. There will be an air of cooperation in all areas of nature.

How will the animals keep the food chain intact and how will they feed their young if they are carnivorous? These animals which have been carnivorous in their past will begin to find their nourishment from plant life. The senseless killing of animals for sport will cease. The eating of flesh will abate and not be the problem it is now. There will be new animals, without intelligence, for the purpose of providing food.

As there will be pockets of technology left intact, much of what is good in the world today will survive. Today's technology will be the seed for future technology. New ideas and concepts will sprout from the old technology. In certain sciences these technologies will be so changed as to be unrecognizable. The technologies which will survive will be helpful to all of mankind.

The body will learn how to revive itself by mental capability. You already know that in the mind are re-energizing qualities. These energies will be understood. The ability to activate these energies will be in each human. The body will go into a deep sleep and be re-energized and reformulate cells for the purpose of healing.

There will be communications with other planets. The beings from other planets will bring much knowledge to you in the healing arts. In the beginning days of the aftertime, beings from other planets will be a great help to mankind. They will reteach you in old and lost arts, such as how to move stones of great weight with your mind. In today's vocabulary it is called levitation. The ability to levitate will be very helpful to you to build great halls and meeting places, to erect homes of new materials and dimension, to aid you in crossing rivers and lakes, and to gather building materials from distances.

These beings will teach the new civilization to govern in righteousness and peace. There will be a blossoming of mental abilities of which you are not aware. These new abilities will help to make the everyday life easier and happier.

The beings of other planets will take the technology left from this era, and teach you how to improve it. They will help you find new forms of energy for locomotion, lighting, communicating and for healing. This will be a time of new beginnings.

Through the communication with spirit will come the ability to plug into the healing energy of the Cosmos. It will be through your mind that healing will take place. The new era will be very much a mental world. You will learn to communicate through your thoughts. You will heal yourself through the ability of your mind. Through mental telepathy, man will be in communication with many worlds: spirit, other planets, dimensions, the animals and even nature herself.

The new species of man will have an understanding of nature, weather patterns, animals, minerals, plants, oceans and oceanic life. Have you not noticed that when the time is right for a new idea to come into life, it does? Have you not noticed that one change brings with it many changes? Now then, what of great changes? Do you not see that great changes bring with them even greater changes?

All will live in harmony. All will be cared for intelligently. The technology of today will seem old, obsolete and archaic. The stories of this era will seem unbelievable to the younger generation. The young will think the old ones do not remember well. Future generations will have no conceptions of hatred, anger and war. The young will not understand the killing of their fellow man because of a mere difference of opinion. They will think all the different religions of today are not true. It will be inconceivable to them to kill because of the differences among man.

Does the new era sound too good to be true? It is not too good. And it is all true. The populations will have been decimated and abated. The people left on earth will have a new will and a new viewpoint. They will see the ignorance of war, the futility of killing because of a difference of religious opinion. The population which will survive will be a new people.

Simply by living through the disasters, vast changes will occur in mankind. No one can live through such events without being changed. No one who survives will remain the same. No matter what they are like at the beginning of the changes, when the Earth begins to settle into its new orbit, the surviving people will already be a new people.

In facing and confronting a disaster head on, each person grows inside himself. The reaction of these people will be spiritual. They will look for God in their lives. They will desire to have the God of the Universe at their sides. They will have eliminated fear from within them. All harsh emotions will have vanished with the storms. The changes will be so great as to change the patterns of life in their DNA forever. Every person who survives physically will be affected.

Every person who does not survive physically will be affected in many other ways. All beings in all worlds will feel some effect from the rotation of the universe.

The survivors will have changed and the changes will be for the better. This is also true of the animals, the plants and the entire world. It is an evolution towards intelligence, peace and love.

The people who do not survive in the physical world will be in the spiritual world. They may be confused at the onset. The changes to their psyches will be just as dramatic. The evolutionary process will be just as great for them.

Evolution is always towards growth. The process of change is always towards growth. All events will be for growth, in the universe, this world and in each individual.

The evolutionary processes are already bearing fruit in the world. For the past hundred or so years, the psychic processes have become more active in man. Some call it a gut feeling or intuition. This is the "psychic nature" being activated in the species. Many call it a "mother's sixth sense."

What is evident is the refining of the sixth sense in mankind. No longer will man live by his five senses: now a sixth sense has been added. This sixth sense has been in you from the beginning of time. Recently it has been activated to an extent that it is now becoming commonplace. Throughout time there have been those who could tap into the psychic. There has been much confusion as to what the psychic is and how it works. It is an inherent sense, much as your sight or hearing. It is the use of the emotional body to see into the unseen, to feel the directions of the Almighty.

The evolutionary process has commenced and is ongoing. Evolution is not a one-time process, but one which is now slowly changing man into the new species. It is doing its work in changing at such a slow pace that it is unnoticeable.

I do not wish to give the impression that there will be no problems for man to face. **It is through a facing of problems that man grows.** But many of the problems of today will be eliminated because angers and hatreds will be eliminated. As always, there will be other issues to face. It is in confronting problems and solving problems that you are strengthened. Although the problems which will face man in the aftertime will be different from today's, there will be peace. Peace in the world and peace in the family.

The beginning of the new era will be quite different from the ending of the same era. This is just, as the ending of this era finds the world quite different from the beginning. Change is the one constant in the universe. There will always be change. It is through change that all things grow.

I wish only to give you a glimpse of the aftertime. It is not the message I came to give. **We must deal with today.** The people who are in the world now need to be prepared.

In the aftertime there will be new energies to use. Such as love, light and many other energies of which you have not yet thought. **You will develop talents which are hidden within you.** You will be able to perform as Jesus did while he was on earth. Remember that he said, "The things I do, you will also."

In this aftertime, man will be different than he is today. He will have many abilities which you do not have now. There will be communication with the spirit world and with other planets in other galaxies and other dimensions. Then earth will become a member of the universe and take her place within the Universal community.

The use of the mind will become commonplace. Your mental abilities will be perfected and expanded. Through concentration you will have more knowledge, more intelligence.

The future holds many wonders and many new abilities for mankind. These abilities can be used for good or for destruction, but man will be harmonious by nature. Drastic changes in nature will bring with them drastic changes in man. Simply surviving the coming events will change man for the better.

10

A Message from Jesus

While we were receiving the messages from Mary, we were told that Jesus would give a chapter to lend creditability to Mary's Message. Jesus told us, "I do not want to preach to the masses, but to give validation to Mother Mary's message. You are to put away your concern with the events which will transpire and look to the hope which we come to give."

TO ALL WHO READ THIS MESSAGE, I come in love and in peace. This is Jesus, who lived on earth at the time of Pontius Pilate. I was born in Bethlehem of Mary and Joseph. I preached around the countryside and asked that each person look within to find his way to Father God. I spoke in parables and in stories to tell the world of God's Love.

These days have been foreseen for some time. I revealed these coming events to John and he wrote the book of *Revelation*. In the book of *Revelation* the story is told in allegory and riddle. John did not have the words to describe the future. He did not have a word for the destruction which the atomic bomb would cause. He did not know how to describe the dumping of chemical waste. No one had heard of chemicals. No one knew about these kinds of waste. So John told as best he could those events as they were shown to him.

The coming Earth-changing events are real and will happen as foretold. The importance of your seeking to unite with God the Father is all the more crucial. It is all the more important that you seek to find Him within you. This is how to connect to the kingdom of heaven.

The message given in these writings is real and is Truth. Mother Mary comes out of love and concern for the people of Earth. She comes to give hope and to give you time to connect to God, Creator of the Universe. I come to clear up some misconceptions about my words.

When I was on earth and giving Truth to the masses, I said over and over that the kingdom of heaven is within you. Many times I told my disciples, and the masses which congregated, to go within to seek the Truth. Enter the closet of your mind, the inner recesses of your heart: this is where to contact God. In this inner closet you will tell God the Father what you will, and openly in public view He will answer.

I said, "When you fast, do not put on a sack cloth and put ashes on your face." To truly fast, do it in private. Do not let anyone know that you are living in a state of prayer and fasting. **The prayers and the fasting are between you and God,** not for the public to see and comment upon. If you are doing the prayers and fasting to be seen and to be heard by men, then this recognition will be your reward. But to truly pray and fast is to go within your mind and heart. In the quietness of your innerself bring your concerns, cares, fears, angers, unforgiveness to God. He will reward you by changing these situations into good. You will find your answer in courage, love, forgiveness, and joy.

Many times while I was on earth, I was asked, "How can we believe this is true?"

I replied, "If you believe me, then you will believe my word."

If for no other reason than I was known to them, they could see, hear, and touch me, and this would be reason enough to believe my word.

But I blessed you of this generation who would believe even if you could not see me. I knew if it was difficult for those who knew me to believe, it would be doubly so for this generation.

How will you believe? By seeing that these events will happen as told by Mother Mary. By sensing the truth which is in these words.

The Gift of Eternal Life

My message to the world was of eternal life, but I see that many churches have placed barriers and requirements on eternal life.

Eternal life is a gift of the Father. **It is through His Love that you have eternal life,** not because you believe in me or profess to my testimony, but simply because of the Great Love God has for His creation. There is nothing you must do to have eternal life. There are no requirements to precede eternal life; there is not one thing which will buy you eternal life. It is yours and it has always been so. From the beginning of time, you have had eternal life. **Each of you has lived before.** There have been lifetimes of work and service given to God. There have been many wasted lifetimes given to your own pleasures also.

In all things God the Father, in His Great Love, has given each person freedom of choice. It is completely up to you to seek God, or to reject Him. It is up to you how you live this and every life.

God is very, very patient. His Love for mankind is so wonderful and so completely unconditional, you cannot begin to hold the concept in your mind.

When I said I came to give life, I did not mean that you did not have life, but that you were not appreciating life. Life is a gift to be appreciated and loved. Today I see among the young and the elderly, hopelessness and despair. It is sad to see how wretched some people are in their minds and hearts. How despondent life has become to many.

The masses continue to look to the outer for satisfaction, to the outer life to fulfill their needs. Now, I see many turning to drugs, alcohol and sensuality to give them satisfaction. Money is not the answer. Life is the answer, an appreciation of life, and of yourself.

The concentration on cars, prestige, money, power, houses and clothes is but a passing fancy. These are things which deteriorate and rot away. But those things of your inner-life—thoughts, loves, forgiveness and feelings—these are the lasting things. This is where your pleasure lies. When you can appreciate the gift of eternal life, you will see Truth. You do not have to become impatient to have it; it is already yours.

You still do not understand that you have life eternally. You still have the concept that this is your only life. You limit the Father. You limit His Love and His care for you. Understand that **this life on earth is but a reflection of your true life,** which is lived in spirit.

I said, "For all who seek, will find the answer, all who ask, it will be given, and to all who knock the door will be opened."

You have asked, you have sought, and you have knocked. Since you have asked you are being answered. The answer is coming to all who have been seeking. To those who have questioned, this is your answer.

These are the last days of which I spoke. This is the "end time" to which I referred. Know that the answer to your survival is in your mind and heart. It is through the kingdom of God that you will receive your answers. See, when faced with the possibilities of these disasters, where are your money, clothes, cars, houses and job? Where is all you have placed value in? How will your money or your profession help you? How will having the right clothes and the best house be of benefit to you? Where will your job get you? How will your education help?

These are things of this world. They are of this world and for this world. In the long run they will not help you with your true life.

Do not look to any other person for your connection to God. This is only available to you through your mind and heart. You must be able to hear and feel God. It will be in your mind that the voice of God will guide you. It will be with your heart that you will feel His Great Love.

Since no one can be your connection to God, neither can you be the connection for a loved one. **It is the responsibility of each individual to seek his own connection to God.** There is not one to a family. It is one per individual.

Others can show you their way to connect. They can teach you their prayers, but in the end each will be on his own. This is why I said, "When people call out here, here is the way to God."

You will know in your heart, because in your heart and through your mind is the only connection made by you to God.

This is not a new way of communicating with me; it has a new name—"automatic writing." This is the method I used to help the disciples write the story of my life. To each I was able to give assistance through this method.

When Paul wrote to the different churches, I was with him. When Timothy answered, I was with him. Nothing is new on earth. What has been, will be again. What was, is and will be.

What today is called "channeling" is not a new way of communicating with God. He has through the ages given His warning of future disasters. He spoke through Ezekiel, Isaiah and the other prophets. He did it then and He can do it now. God is alive, God is well, and God is still creating.

These predictions are all true. David wrote about this possibility in the Psalms, where he said, "Even though the earth be moved, I will trust in you my God."

Revelation

I would like for you to read the last book of the Bible—
Revelation, the one in which John foresaw the coming changes.
He describes these in very flowery and dramatic language.
When he uses the terms which describe monsters, it will seem
like this is happening. It will seem that you are being overtaken
by these things. He is using analogies to describe conditions.
This tells you what will happen. Remember that this describes,
and is not the absolute.

It is understandable that you do not comprehend this
book. It is written in allegory and in riddle.

The seven churches are representative of the major religions. The seven angels of these churches represent the membership of these different religions.

This is a call to religions to remember that it is not with
good works, or with poverty or with anything on the outside
which will get you into a good connection with God the Father.
Many religions preach good works; they are very interested in
helping the less fortunate. This is good, but this alone will not
satisfy the spiritual need.

There are those religions which ask for donations and seek
to have much gold and money in their vaults. These worldly
goods will not be of value to your spiritual life.

Now, this is how to understand the messages to the seven
churches, or to the seven angels, who are representative of the
membership of these particular religions.

In the prologue, you see that it is stated, "Your sins are
freed by his blood."

This is a way of saying that I came to give you truth, to free
all people from misconceptions which inhibit. Sin is simply
another way of saying a "spiritual mistake." The biggest spiritual mistake is to hold on to the misconceptions which limit you
spiritually, not to question or seek the answers from God.

Revelation 1:7 reads, "Look, he is coming with the clouds,
and every eye will see him."

Your connection to God is coming with the clouds. "Clouds" denote the thoughts of man. "Every eye" is speaking of the inner eye, the eye which allows you to see in truth.

(Revelation 4:)

The seven spirits of God are Divine Love, Divine Light (which includes illumination, ideas, all types of light), Divine Power, Divine Wisdom, Divine Will, Divine Life, and Divine Order. Through these seven spirits, God is able to keep the Universe in a state of creative being.

The four creatures represent the people from the four corners of the world: east, west, north, and south. All the eyes represent the inner eye of the people. The reason the creatures are praising God night and day is that someone is always praising God somewhere on earth. The twenty-four thrones surrounding the Throne represent the different dimensions, levels and planes. The elders are the inhabitants of these dimensions, levels and planes.

(Revelation 5–6:)

The scroll represents the history of man. There is writing on both sides of the scroll because you are at the end of an era. The scroll is used up. The first seal represents the time of the crusades, when men went out to conquer the Holy Land. His intentions were good, so it is represented by the white horse, but intentions are not everything.

The second seal represents the time of the inquisition and the witch hunts, when people were put to death for their beliefs.

The third seal represents the sending forth of priests to bring gold and pagan tribes of people to the Church, as when man discovered the new world.

The fourth seal represents the dark ages and the time of the great plagues, when death was all about the lands.

The fifth seal represents the purging of Jews, during your world war, and all people in these 2000 years who have lost their lives because of their beliefs.

The sixth seal represents the atomic bomb, the killing of millions of innocent people, many who had no control over the injustices of their nation. It is also representative of these "end times" when storms will begin to lash the world, when earthquakes will be in every part of the world.

The seventh seal has not yet been shown completely.

(Revelation 7:1-8)

The 144,000 people who have the seal on them and the four angels on the four corners of the world are the people who are prepared to face these last days on earth, the ones with the Seal of God on them. They will not be harmed. There are multitudes who will grow spiritually because of the tribulation and disasters which they will survive. Now I speak of survival not as physical, but more of spiritual survival. These are the people who are seeking God with earnestness and sincerity of heart.

The 144,000 are representative of the people who belong to the major religions, who through their religions have found a close union with God. They have gone to the heart of the matter and found their connection to God. The seventh seal is opening now. It is the "end time," the time when all storms are let loose. Earthquakes and volcanos will be active all around the world. See how *Revelation* is a story about the end times? See how these many creatures, numbers and allegories represent something?

(Revelation 7:8-17)

Now as you read, there is a multitude in white robes. These are the people who have found their God connection all alone. They have been able to see past the religiousness, rituals and creeds of the different religions to God. They are the ones who found their God connection in their heart and mind as it should be. They have not faltered but have persevered in searching out the truth. These are the great multitudes who have put aside their differences and seen the creation of God.

Understand that the seventh seal is not yet completed. It is your near future. The words in this allegory sound very frightening because there will be much fear in those who are on earth. The earth-mind consciousness has already been steeped in much fear. It is this fear which will paralyze the populations of the world.

Seven is the number in which God created the world and all on it in the allegory of creation. It is the number in which God works. So seven angels and seven trumpets are simply indicating a completion. The completion of this era, this civilization and these times as they are now known.

(Revelation 8:1-5)

The angel offering prayers is happening now. The Saints, and all the people in other planes and on other planets, are now offering prayers for you on earth. The amount of prayers sound like thunder, lightning, and earthquakes.

The first angel brought hail and fire, and a third of the world was burned, a third of the trees, and a third of the green grass. Do you not understand that you have already depleted a third of the Earth with chemicals? Through the abuse of chemicals you have destroyed a third of the earth, trees and grass, and now because of the multiplying population, entire forests are being burned, not just in one part of the world but all over the globe.

(Revelation 8:8)

The second angel had "something like a huge mountain, all ablaze," thrown into the sea. This symbol represents the huge mountain of trash, chemicals and nuclear waste which is now being dumped into the seas. It has destroyed a third of the sea and the sea creatures are dying. The ships represent the commerce of seafood and that is being destroyed.

With the third angel, a great star, blazing like a torch, falls from the sky and a third of the rivers and springs of water are destroyed and turned bitter. Many people die from the waters. Can you not see that you have polluted your drinking water with chemicals and nuclear waste? This is a worldwide problem. It is one which affects all waters of the world. These chemicals are being produced in other nations which are considered backward and ignorant. You in this country are the foolish ones, because as you destroy other nations, you are also destroying your environment, your planet.

The fourth angel is about to sound its trumpet. This will be asteroids which will bombard the solar system. Your nation and others will try to deflect the incoming asteroids with nuclear bombs. This act will simply serve to affect one third of the sky, the stars, planets and the sun. This will happen soon. The asteroid belt is already in turmoil. There have been several asteroids which have entered your solar system. These are all sizes, large and small.

(Revelation 8:13)

The eagle flying in midair calling out "Woe! Woe! Woe to the inhabitants of the earth," is representative of people like

Ruth Montgomery, Edgar Cayce, Nostradamus, this writer, and others who have been prophesying these coming events. These days will be a frightening, terrifying time on earth only if you are lost and feel disconnected from God.

The remainder of the book of *Revelation* explains the coming events, but you have a better guide in Mother Mary because she has given you her predictions and the times in which these events will occur.

Also understand that by living through these events you will progress in spirit one hundred times one thousand. It is by eliminating your fear and depending on God, me or the help of the Brotherhood of God that you will find solace, peace and help. **Now is the time for you to connect to God.** Now is the time to put aside all doubts and believe me.

(Revelation 9:1)

The fifth angel will sound his horn and "the star was given the key to the shaft of the Abyss." An abyss is a very deep pit, much as the ones in the bottom of the oceans, but this simply describes the events that Mother Mary has given you which will happen in the next five years. This time period will see storms, earthquakes and climatic changes. These words simply describe what it will seem like.

The locust are the storms. The stingers on their tails are the turmoil which people will feel. With each storm which increases in size, there will be much fear added to the earth-mind consciousness. With each earthquake and the appearance of new volcanos, the sky will seem dark. People will be tortured with fear, but not many will lose their lives.

The sixth angel sounds his horn. The great earthquakes will begin and the spewing of sulfur through the increased volcanic activity. This will be the time Mother Mary has given you which is 1995 and thereabout.

Now, when John took the little scroll and ate it, the taste was like honey in the mouth, but in the stomach it was bitter. This means that when you know of the end times and are prophesying to others, as Mother Mary is, the news will be sweet in their mouth.

At first, many will say, "You are lucky to be psychic," or they will admire your abilities. But when they think on the message and hear the message, they will turn against you. The role you are playing will be a bittersweet one. It will bring fame and infamy.

The seventh angel represents the time of the actual turning of the planet. The twenty-four elders are representative of the beings from other worlds who will come to lift many of you off the planet. The symbol is the temple of heaven which opened to reveal the ark of the covenant. It is God's way of saying many will survive on earth, but I will assure you that many survive because I will allow the beings to gather people and take them away from the last turmoil. Many will be saved, not because of money, power or any other worldly matter, but because of the sincerity and the earnestness with which they are seeking God.

It will not be apparent that these people are seekers. Many will seem uneducated, poor and dirty. But know that those with the Seal of God will be lifted.

Some of the ones left on earth with the seal will survive. But others with the seal will go on to spirit.

Now when you read the story of the pregnant woman and the dragon, realize that the woman is Mother Earth. It could be said Mother Earth is pregnant with the child of a new era. The dragon represents the old fears, hates, hostilities and greed of the race consciousness, or the earth-mind consciousness. This earth-mind consciousness wants to survive, to enter the new era with all its fears, hates, wars, hostilities and greed. God will not permit it. God will not permit these strong, negative emotions to continue to wage havoc on earth in the new era.

The beast of the earth had power to cause fire to come down from heaven. Through signs and powers this beast gained much. Of those who had the mark of the beast, 666 were allowed to sell and trade. Many people today think this is the mark of the devil. To such an extent is this believed that many on earth today in all parts of the world are worshipping the devil. They say, "He has power to give riches and to protect us."

The devil is the race consciousness of greed, power, and wealth from ill-gotten gains. It is drugs and addictions of all kinds. It is abuse of children, women and men. This race consciousness says it is all right to kill and slay in sacrifice. It is the belief in the occult, and by this I mean in the hidden, those who believe that in the hidden realms are greater powers than God. This is the war which the so-called religions are waging now against the devil. The war of who is right, which church is the way.

Remember I said while on earth, "In the last days many would come saying here, here this is the way, this is the truth."

But I told you, "I am the way, the truth, and the life."

It is through the use of the words "I am," that you will find your connection within to God. In your mind and heart you are shown truth and life. Only through your God-Mind connection will you be guided. In this way, through each individual, the truth, the way, and the life will be given.

These preachers who are shouting from their pulpits about the war with the devil are simply playing into the belief of evilness. They are aiding the race consciousness which wishes to survive. These preachers bring fear, hostility and these kinds of emotion to the people. They preach fear instead of love. They preach that the devil has much power, but this only gives this concept more power.

When you find that you are truly connected to God from within, then you will eliminate fear, hostility and such. Not by power or might, but by the Word of God, by taking into your life the Love of God and the Word of God. By accepting the Goodness of God, you have your salvation. You do not have salvation as the Christian religions denote this word, but salvation which comes from knowing the truth, the relief which is felt by connecting to God in your heart and mind. There is no big devil, except in your thoughts. There is no great war occurring in heaven, except in the minds of men.

The 144,000 who were found blameless are those who have found their connection to God. They are the ones who have brought their whole selves to God through their hearts and minds. They have given themselves totally to God. They have brought their fears, angers, hostilities, greed and all manner of thoughts to the altar. God has changed these depleting emotions into love, forgiveness, charity, hope and courage. They have the Seal of God on them. They are sincere in seeking to find God. Now, there are three angels who fly in midair. One has the eternal gospel, the other proclaims the fallen beast and the third calls to those with the mark of the beast. These are the times in which you are living. You have with you the gospel, the method of communicating with God. Today there are many preachers giving the gospel as they see it, but **be aware the eternal gospel can only come to you through your mind and heart.** You need no longer be afraid of the beast, because you recognize that he is an illusion. He is nothing unless you make him something. So you can tell others that there is no devil; it is a fallacy. It is not real. This belief in a devil will deter you from your spiritual goals. You will lose your spiritual growth if you continue to believe in the devil.

The harvest of the earth is the time when people will still be able to find their connection to God. In the future time when there are earthquakes and destruction, many will begin to seek God with sincerity of heart and mind. This is the harvest.

The symbol of seven angels with the seven plagues and the seven bowls of God's wrath represents the last turning of the Earth. For as you read these passages you will see the event in allegory. It even states that this will be like no earthquake ever felt by man before.

The fall of Babylon is the fall of the trade empire upon which nations have built their worth. It is world trade in paper stocks, paper money, and in goods of all kinds. As there will be pockets of technology left, many will weep and cry for the days in which the world was connected by satellite, computers and commerce.

The great multitude and the twenty-four elders represent the beings on other planets, in other dimensions, levels and planes. Those represent all who are concerned for people of Earth, and all who are praying for you on earth.

In the new era you will have 1000 years of peace because the devil consciousness has been eliminated. There will be no fear, anger or hostility.

The first resurrection is the resurrection of your spiritual growth. It will be for the people who reincarnate in the new era to live peacefully, to fulfill their spiritual goals with alacrity.

The judging of the dead is the calling up of those who are in suspended animation. They will be given the chance to rectify their mistakes. It will be judged as to the sincerity of their hearts and minds at that time. If they are lacking, they will return to this turned off state for 1000 years, because one who is not progressing spiritually will not be allowed to remain conscious.

The new Jerusalem is the new era. It is the time of peace on earth. It will be a new and mighty time on earth. This will be the time of completions. It will be the time of great progress on earth and in the spiritual realm. That is the reason it is a time of celebration.

Each soul will be measured and all who are worthy by the sincerity of their seeking of God, will live in peace and progress spiritually. The book of *Revelation* says "Jesus is coming."

Yes, I, Jesus will walk and live among you on earth, in full, open view. There will be communication with the spirit world, and those who are deemed worthy will progress in all levels. You will not have the same needs as you do now. You will be a new man and a new woman. New times and new thoughts will prevail. I will give personal guidance to all.

My aim is that you see the hope and the love in which this prophesy was given. Take hope into full account in your life, your inner-life, now. It gives you the impetus to seek God with all your heart, all your mind and with all your might. In so doing, by prayer and meditation, you will be prepared to survive unto the end, to survive and to endure these last times with courage, hope, and love. This is my prayer and this is my hope: that all progress in spirit, that no one be turned off for the next 1000 years because it will be a glorious time. These will be wonderful, peaceful lives you will lead on earth.

I came to give you the hope of eternal life, the understanding that you do not have to do anything to obtain eternal life. You already have it so you can put away fear, anger, hate and greed, these emotions which deplete your creative energies.

I came to tell you the Truth: all you have to do is seek God the Father with a sincere heart and earnest mind; that the only way to find God is through your thoughts and with your feelings. You can have peace; you can have love now. You do not have to wait until the aftertime. All is available to you now, today.